A Mountain to Climb

A MOUNTAIN TO CLIMB

PAT TURNER MITCHELL

A MOUNTAIN TO CLIMB

iUniverse books may be ordered through booksellers or by contacting:

iUniverse
1663 Liberty Drive
Bloomington, IN 47403
www.iuniverse.com
1-800-Authors (1-800-288-4677)

ISBN: 978-1-5320-0473-5 (sc)
ISBN: 978-1-5320-0472-8 (e)

Library of Congress Control Number: 2016913252

Print information available on the last page.

iUniverse rev. date: 08/25/2016

This book is in memory of my parents,
Edith Rae McKinney and David Ellis Turner,
my husband, Jack Mitchell, and all those who came
before us. It is in honor of my brother, James E. Turner
and his wife, Revonda; my sister, Janice Turner Cline
and her husband, John and all their families.

The line fades

Between sky and mountain when day falls to darkest night,

Between man and woman as we merge in love,

Between war and peace when we

Lose our way.

CONTENTS

My first book "Lifted to the Shoulders of a Mountain" was about my maternal grandparents, their families and their stories handed down to us as they lived in what became Little Switzerland. N. C. This book, "A Mountain to Climb" continues their story but will focus on their youngest child, Edith McKinney, and her family as they lived in Valdese, N. C.

It begins with my paternal family, my dad's story, David Ellis Turner. My intent in both books is to bring to life those who brought us to life. It will be our story, too; a look back at our beginning. But this book became my personal journey to understand the choices my dad made in his life.

My paternal grandfather, Junius Pinkney (June) Turner, was very real but he died in Salisbury, N. C. when my dad was only fifteen months old. My sister, Janice, and I have found census records and death certificates which give his and his family's addresses, type of work, places and cause of death. In this book I imagine their story from these facts.

I was born when my mother was nineteen and my dad almost twenty and have clear memories of them and my brother and me growing up against the background of World War II and my sister as she grew up after this traumatic time. Their story here gives my perception and that of those others who left records of the events that shaped my parent's early marriage and what I learned from family letters that were written before and after I was born.

In my research of that time I asked for and received records of our dad's short time in the Navy and Merchant Marine service during this war. I received a large envelope of them which included forms and letters written and signed by both Mother and Dad.

As in my previous book I have a few minor fictional characters and I have taken some liberties imagining what the actual characters might have done or said in their circumstances. A story line that I weave through this book plays into actual experiences (dreams) that my sister, Janice, and I had that I write about in Chapter 15. One that makes me believe that we are closely related to the earth beneath our feet; that its history and traumas leave their memories of times past with us.

These experiences were brought home to me when I read "Exploring the Geology of the Carolinas" by Kevin G. Steward and Mary-Russell Roberson. He was associate professor of geology sciences at UNC, Chapel Hill and she was a freelance science writer when it was published by UNC Press in 2007. They explored South Mountain State Park in 2003 after Hurricane Hugo went through in 1989. Because of a heavy deluge of rain, they were able to see a great slide of rocks, mostly metamorphic. "When you encounter that much metamorphic rock at once, it is evidence of a large regional event, such as a collision between plates." If this area has evidence that it may have been the end of our continent about 300 plus million years ago then my sister's and my dreams make sense.

I hope you enjoy reading "A Mountain to Climb."

PROLOGUE

1943

David is sleeping, alone in his seat aboard a train. According to his family he often talked and walked in his sleep in these early years; it is likely his muttering would have kept the seat beside him vacant. His dreams are troubled. He hasn't contacted his wife, Edith, that he has been medically discharged from the Navy and sent home.

He is dreaming now of an earlier time, seeing a winding road curving around a high mountain in 1934 when he first met her. He saw young men moving over the bare ground, digging terraces to protect young saplings others are planting. They were trying to replace trees that were logged some years before, leaving the mountains vulnerable to erosion and slides. He also wanted to be part of this group of 'fixers' back when the government stepped up to the plate during the big depression. This dream couldn't be, though. Not for David anyway; he was struggling to climb his own mountain.

David knows when he is dreaming, else he couldn't be floating above everything and everybody. In these dreams he is only observing, not taking part. It is like life excludes him.

He may have dreamed about his hero, the man whose death pushed him to enlist in the Navy. David wanted to live up to the life he thinks this man could have lived; maybe then his vivid memory of this tragedy may be laid to rest. This isn't a dream but a walking nightmare. It is one he can't talk about, not with his family or others that are close to him.

He opens his eyes as he feels the train slow and his coach jerk into place; he begins unfolding his lean body from the seat as the train pulls into the station. Reaching for his duffle bag he can feel his muscles stretch, reminding him of the strenuous hours he spent sculpting his body while strengthening his muscles. In his mind someone who looks strong would be strong.

As he steps out into the twilight it's dark enough to see faint lights close by. Some people are still at their supper. His eyes take in the small wooden station with railroad tracks going east and west connecting to the north and the south. He looks at the tracks, hopeful maybe, or wondering if he should turn around and leave.

While the war is raging the Navy has sent him home. They gave him just enough money to travel from Pensacola to Charlotte where he had enlisted. He is thankful he had enough money to get home.

He fingers the carved soap animals in his coat pocket; "Keeps your hands busy," the hospital staff told him, handing him a bar of soap and a carving tool. Maybe his little son, Jim, would like to take these into his bathwater. After all they would float since they were made from bars of Ivory soap.

Looking towards the dark recreation center David is reminded of the barbells that he bought when he took the Charles Atlas Course. He wishes he could go there first. He shivers in his Navy pea coat then straightens his shoulders. He'll need to find work to take care of Edith and the children, finding a way to hold his head up while able men are at war. There is a constant reminder since you can see this war up close now in newsreels.

He thinks of his brother, Edgar, who enlisted in the Army in 1930, a year or two after he graduated high school in the orphanage. David has just come to know him but worries about Edgar; he can't do anything but worry, though. He hopes to spend more time with him and his sister, Beulah, who were sent to an orphanage when David was just a baby.

His demeanor is grave when he looks at the dark silhouette of the low mountain range giving a backdrop to the town. He has grown up close by these South Mountains.

He steps away from the empty station and starts for home. It will take him longer to walk this distance now. His special shoes take some of his weight off his damaged arches but he steps carefully, wondering how far he can walk.

His mind begins to tumble the muddle of events from the past months: the memory of Edith coming to see him in Florida, his friends so goggled eyed to see her in the flesh. They had talked about moving their family down. It seemed possible while holding her in his arms. Then he remembers the other girls he held. Shaking his head, he stops to light a cigarette, a new habit for him.

His mind skips to the time at the Navy base when he went up in the bi-plane and an engine fell off as they skimmed the tops of waves. His buddy jumped out of the plane but David stayed with the pilot as he brought her in and landed on the water. He would keep that story to himself. David was good at that.

Edith wondered why he couldn't share his feelings with those he loved the most but then she probably knew the answer. He can't let people know he might be afraid, that he is vulnerable. He remembers those days not too long ago; a little boy in a family that didn't have time to give to him. You have to put up a brave front, always.

Having to leave school early to work had proved to be a big stumbling block in the Navy. But he is a husband now, a father, and he thinks it's too late for school. He is breathing deeply as he walks along. He passes the road that would take him past his mother, Ollie's, house. Down a hill, up a hill, he was getting closer to his reality. Could a strong body carry him while he trembled with his lack of confidence?

David and Edith Turner, 1942 (Home on leave)

CHAPTER 1

*T*he doctor walked into David's hospital room carrying a file in his hand. He glanced around, noting that the other beds were empty. He pulled up a chair beside David's bed and sat.

"Well, young man, I need to hear your story. According to your entry physical you came into the Navy with a minor condition of flat feet Pes planus, 2nd degree. This seemed to become more of a problem when you began exercising in your training."

Report: History of flat feet all his life but no pain or trouble with them until two weeks after he reported to duty. First began suffering pain with feet after about an hour of exercise. Gradually became more severe and extended up legs until he became unable to perform his duties because of pain.

Physical examination: Bilateral flaccid depression of the longitudinal arches. Complete pronation of both feet on weight bearing. Tender to pressure fascia and the calves of each leg.

"You also have recurring asthma attacks. Your therapy is coming along but it may take some time for you to get back to moving like you used to. We will remove the bindings on your feet before long but you will need special shoes and maybe further treatment."

He met David's eyes. "I know you experienced pain when you were jumping from a height, landing on hard ground, during your training. I wonder if you played football or other sports in school, maybe had pain in your feet when you ran?"

David shook his head no; he didn't have pain. "I loved playing football. I didn't play long, though. I had to leave school to get a job."

"Tell me about your family then."

David reached for his robe and stood while he put it on. He had special slipper-shoes he put on while his feet were strengthening. "Sir, may I walk a little as I talk?" At the doctor's nod, he began telling his story.

"My step-daddy was the only dad I knew. He had a son, Lewis, whose mama died about the same time as my own dad. Mama married him about two years later. I was too young to remember much of these days but he took us to his home near the South Mountains. It wasn't long before Mama was expecting a baby. That first one died but she had four more."

David retied his robe with a jerk. "He never had much time for me. He didn't have much time for Mama and their children either. Times were hard. I considered him a bully to me. It came to blows one time. I won."

David sat in a chair rubbing his knuckles. "I married when I was nineteen but didn't know much about how it was meant to be."

He looked up. "I wonder if my step-daddy rubbed off on me."

The doctor started. "No, I would never hurt my wife; not physically, anyway. You can believe that."

He didn't mention his stepfather's philandering ways. Maybe David thought this was the way of things in a marriage.

Left: Front: Ellis Leander, Leathie, Charity Kisiah Turner.
Back: Unknown (Leathie's parents?)
Right: Ollie King and Junius Pinckney Turner, 1910

In 1916 women are important. They are brave, have dreams, manage families, cook, clean, and have babies; one, three, six, however many babies come until their tired bodies give up. Some die in childbirth but some others are left to raise their children alone. (On May 1, 1916 my dad, David Ellis Turner, was born to Ollie King and Junius Pinckney Turner.)

As the sunrays came through the window, dust motes rode on a beam of light accenting the mound of her stomach. The muscles contracted with her moan that climbed into a scream. Hands spread Ollie's legs apart, lifting her buttocks as the doctor's hands received the baby. It was a boy.

She sank into the mattress, hoping it would swallow her up. 'What will I do with another child and June so frail?' is what she was thinking. Ollie opened her eyes and looked up at her husband. He was leaning on a cane but stepped back as her friend, Eleanor, laid a swaddled baby in her arms. She closed her eyes, squeezing tears down her cheeks.

A clean sheet was folded and slipped beneath her hips while her friend pulled the soiled bedding away, dropping them in a pail before covering Ollie. Two little faces appeared beside the bed, leaving their grandparents standing in the doorway. Edgar was in first grade, Beulah was almost old enough to start school. Gulping back her tears, Beulah turned her face to her dad, hugging his legs. She is so tenderhearted; seeing her mama in distress was new to her.

The doctor cleared his throat, and all eyes turned to him. He looked at June who was trying to stand straight but couldn't manage. "Mr. Turner, I believe you have a healthy son. The birth took a while but your wife held up. How are you making out?"

"I'm not working, Doc, so money's tight. I'll need to talk to the railroaders, to see if they have something I can do 'til I strengthen some. Can you wait a little for your pay?"

The doctor took his stethoscope from his pocket. "Sit down. Let me listen to your lungs. Your chest took a hard blow when your "Indian" hit the fence. It didn't help when you went end over end, breaking your leg to boot. I call you lucky, myself."

He looked down while listening to ominous sounds coming through his instrument. It wouldn't do for his young family to know how dire their situation could become. In this year of 1916 miracles seldom happened.

"Mr. Turner, do you have help here? You'll need someone to cook and help you look after the children until Mrs. Turner can be up and about."

His parents stepped into the room. "We can see to this family until Ollie is up, I reckon," Charity Kiziah Turner said.

June's dad, Ellis Leander Turner, had turned his meat market in Statesville over to another son. He didn't have the strength now to keep it open since he was in failing health. He and Charity had settled here in Salisbury just to be close to June and Ollie. They offered them part of a nice house they bought on West Franklin. It made it easier for June but Ollie didn't care much for his folks.

June loved that house. A big old Elm tree shaded the back yard where the children played while Ollie went about hanging the wash on a clothes line. He had strung it between two poles he had set up. He liked to lean back against the Elm and work on his new found Indian Motor Cycle, content with his world.

Ollie looked up, still cradling her infant son. "Eleanor here can help out today. My sister is coming tonight. She'll stay a few days. We should be all right."

She reached her free hand towards their little girl. "Now Beulah, dry your tears and come look at your new brother." She looked at June. "We'll call him David, after your granddad."

With just a few words she told his parents she didn't need their help; then to take the sting out of her words she named their new son after June's grandfather. Looking back the pattern seemed to begin with him, David Turner, who died a Confederate prisoner way up in Pennsylvania when June's dad was 3 years old.

It is easier to see that day now; anyone can find the account in a book listing our troops that served so many years back. June's granddad was in Company F. 55th Regiment North Carolina, coming in from Cleveland County, enlisting February 23, 1863. It wasn't likely he had much choice about 'enlisting' at that time in the war, though. And on July 1, 1863 the men were waking to another muggy day, unsure if they would have food to fill their grumbling stomachs. Soon they were scrambling to get their ragged shoes, then their rifles, starting a zigzag march towards Gettysburg. David Turner fell forward in the tall grass, watching enemy troops all around, waiting for the signal to attack. Hot, thirsty, too tired to think of their stomachs, they marched to their death or capture.

According to the record he ended up in an abandoned railroad bed with his fellow doomed Confederates, too tired to run or try to climb the steep bank. He was taken prisoner and marched to Fort Delaware, then a hospital in Chester, Pennsylvania where he died August 2, 1863, from dysentery or something like it. His wife, Agnes Bolick Turner would raise her children without a father.

June limped to Ollie's side, taking her hand. She looked down thinking he had strong, capable hands. Ollie never said but she loved his hands.

They had courted in a cemetery. It was a private place unless there was a digging crew or family visiting a grave site in the early evening and the closest to an acceptable but discrete place that the mill town afforded. The benches sat under trees whose branches protected them some when it rained. (A story told to me by my dad.)

June had come here to Catawba County to work in the mill since it was close to his home near Wittenberg in Alexander County. Ollie had come from Gaston County, near Cherryville, to do the same. June wondered why she left home to get a job since Gastonia has many mills. Now he knew she came to be closer to her sisters who lived nearby.

Ollie King was a tiny girl. Not even five feet tall, she could easily walk under June's out-stretched arm. In the early twilight he would lift her to a bench so he could better hold her in his arms.

A comet streaked across the sky the night she agreed to marry him. June felt it was for them alone even when he heard people talk about seeing Haley's Comet that April of 1910. This is because his granddad, David, told Grandma Agnes this phenomenon would mean something to him when it came again. She wondered, like he did, what that cryptic statement meant. It seems this is what his daddy had told him when he told the story of the 1834 comet that came around about every 76 years.

Although June's granddad wasn't alive to see this comet April 20, 1910, he likely did see it from his vantage point and maybe the connection to June's youngest son and his future.

June had to marry Ollie. He couldn't contain his will to have her. All the young ladies were kept secure in their living quarters, curfew coming early. It wouldn't do for a bleary eyed girl to have her arm chewed off by machinery or be sent home in disgrace. No sir. These young ladies were protected, until they married anyway. They paid no mind to what was happening outside their small world. June moved them in with his parents in Statesville when they married and he needed to find a new job.

His mechanical ability helped him get a good job at the railroad shop at Spencer, near Salisbury, and close by Statesville where his father had his meat market. Ellis had just bought the house in Salisbury and it was close enough to Spencer. Salisbury had a strong Lutheran Community, which would help June's mother feel at home. June settled his new wife in Salisbury and his mother and dad soon joined them. Their son was born, then a daughter. Now they had David, too.

But before he was born June found a smashed up motorcycle in a trash pile. He knew he had found a treasure. Always tinkering with old, discarded machinery he searched for parts, bargaining until they were his. He was soon blasting down the dirt roads. Sometimes he explored Salisbury.

There was money in Salisbury back in that time. Beautiful Victorian style homes were built sitting back from tree lined streets close by down town where the well-to-do could walk to their banks or stores in town.

June walked around the area close by where the Confederate Prison used to be, between South Long and South Lee Streets, where an old abandoned cotton factory housed the early prisoners of war. It was close to the railroad tracks that brought prisoners from Pennsylvania, Maine, and New York, captured from many battle sites. The cemetery, where so many of these prisoners are buried, isn't far from the prison. He walked here thinking of his own grandfather, not knowing where he died or where his remains might be.

Life was good in the foothills in that day. More people were leaving their farms to work but usually not too far from home. Ellis Leander was born on a farm in Cleveland County but it was near Wittenberg in Alexander County where his wife grew up. Parts of Alexander, Caldwell and Catawba counties joined close by here. Crops still put food on the table, supplemented by town jobs. The factories and mills were moving down since northern states were setting up laws to protect workers. Not down here, though. The mills were working good hours then.

Most didn't notice the pall that hung over them. Like the dirty fog from a coal fire pollutes the air, war news from Europe began to erode the underground of society here.

As it often happens this erosion won't be noticed by many people until the ground falls from beneath them. Our country didn't expect we would be in this war and few had paid attention when our mills began turning out fabric that would become uniforms.

In this year of 1916 war wasn't close yet because we didn't know those fighting and news was slow in coming. Troops were fighting in places foreign to most. They may read about it but it didn't worry them; their world was a stable place, in their mind anyway. (They didn't know then that T. E. Lawrence, known later as Lawrence of Arabia, fighting for the British in the deserts of Arabia, would write a book intimating that the decisions made at the end of this war would set up more friction with the Arab world. As we will see this would continue throughout the 20th Century and beyond.) ["Seven Pillars of Wisdom" published by Doubleday, Doran & Company, Inc. in 1935]

On the day of June's accident little Edgar walked to school as usual. His mother wouldn't let him ride the 'Indian' with him. Beulah was helping Ollie in the house. The day that changed the tilt of their axis was ordinary.

"Mama, what causes your belly to be so big?"

Ollie looked up, making another swipe with the soapy cloth on the wooden table. She rinsed the cloth in the pan of water and continued wiping the surface. Swallowing, she kept silent for a moment wondering what to tell her. Before she knew it, this child would be grown up with a baby growing in her belly.

"Do you remember the time before Eleanor had little Johnny, before he was born?"

Beulah's eyes widened. "Is that why she had such a big belly, Mama? Why, do babies grow in your belly? No. That Johnny was too big. How did he get out?"

"Well, when the time comes, a baby comes out, no matter what."

Just then someone pounded on the door. They both turned to see a policeman standing with his arm raised to hit the jam beside the screened door again. Ollie raised a hand and covered her mouth, pulling Beulah behind her. She walked to the door feeling her daughter tugging on her dress. The news would be bad. She knew that.

She and June's parents were taken to see the broken man lying trussed like a turkey in the hospital; on their way home Ollie turned her head away as she passed what was left of the twisted metal that was such a joy to him.

David was just about fifteen months old when June died. His crushed chest made easy pickings when typhoid came along. The doctors in Salisbury had been trying inoculations to control this dread disease. Too bad they weren't available to common folk back then. No one knew where he picked it up but it overcame him well enough.

His dad moved him to Whitehead-Stokes Sanatorium located at the corner of North Fulton and West Liberty in town so he couldn't pass this terrible sickness to his young family. He lay there nine days in the awful heat and on the 13th of August, 1917, he drew his last breath.

June didn't think about this place where he lay being close to where the Confederate Prison used to be back in the 1860's. Northern soldiers were imprisoned there and as the war was ending more were transported here; many died in the last months of the War Between the States. I wonder if he was aware of the essence of those spirits on this holy ground?

David was such a funny looking child, looking out at the world with big round eyes. He crawled as fast as he could from one target to the next. Sometimes he paused as if listening, looking up instead of at what was going on around him. There was always plenty going on.

Ollie wouldn't listen to her in-laws. Her mother-in-law, a Kiziah, was of German stock with her mother born a Herman. She had led the Turner family to the Lutheran Church, too. God was only above cleanliness. Ollie took to their ways but wanted to take her children close by her sisters in Burke County. She needed familiar faces around her. Would they understand the plan she was working up in her head?

'The world is at war for God's sake. People are making the best decisions they can. Why, a mother has to do this every day. The welfare of my children is at stake,' she was thinking.

Left to right: Beulah, David and Edgar Turner, 1917

CHAPTER 2

Ollie waited until she arrived at her sister's house. Lottie and her husband were only able to give the Turner's one room to put their belongings and to rest at night. She would need money to help with groceries and what little she had wouldn't last long. Beulah cried for her daddy while Edgar tried to comfort her and keep a brave face. Little David took his food at Ollie's breast.

Lottie and their friend, Eleanor, had made the contact for her. A lady from the orphanage would come sometime this week.

Wringing her hands, she wondered 'Would they take both Beulah and Edgar? Could she actually see them walk out the door? There was David to care for. She couldn't give up. But would they survive being torn from their mother, too?' Ollie's jumbled thoughts ran through her head. She put her hands to her throat and the floor came up to meet her.

A lady from the orphanage came. She would take Edgar and Beulah if Ollie would follow the rules: no visits or contact of any kind for the first six months, clothes and packages must be sent in care of the orphanage. The lady hoped tangible goods would be sent to help defray expenses of their care. The children couldn't stay together. The rules were made for the child, she said, to help them get used to another home away from loved ones. Ollie knew that Edgar would be determined to survive, even though it would break his heart. Beulah. Beulah would have no one to help her through the long nights.

She would always remember her confused expression when Edgar took her hand and led her to the orphanage car. Ollie had to turn away for fear she would cry out.

The wonder was why she would rather put their children in an orphan's home rather than let Mr. and Mrs. Turner help her. Maybe she thought she would be better able to keep control of her children, maybe bring them home when times were better. She had often turned her back when they offered assistance, though.

Ellis Leander and Charity returned to Alexander County some five years after their son's death where they would live out their lives close by where their family started out. Mr. Turner died while riding out in his buggy on a sunny day in March of 1930, eight years later. His wife was sitting on the porch waiting for him when his horse trotted up to the steps and stopped. She thought he was asleep with his hat tipped down over his face slumped back in the corner of the seat. It would be sixteen more years before she joined him.

———— ∽∞∾ ————

Ollie was thinking about going back to a mill job; David was old enough to wean. She figured she could find someone in her family who could keep him since those with a husband might be able to stay home with their children. There were several mills in the Waldensian town close by Lottie. Then she met a widower with a young son about the age of David.

Ollie had high hopes when she met him. After all, his family was some of the first settlers in the county and they each had a young son to look after. They liked what they saw in each other, too. Before they married she even hoped he would want to bring Beulah and Edgar home. Her hopes were raised after telling him her plans. He didn't say a word and to Ollie that was positive. Little did she know.

Within months of their marriage, she was expecting a child. With two toddlers and a baby, while trying to please her husband, her plans soon scattered. All Ollie could do was drag herself from the kitchen stove, to the wash pot, to a screaming boy, then baring her breast for the baby.

Then she noticed that David was becoming less demanding. It wasn't usual for a child his age but instead of reaching out with his little hand, crying out when he wanted something, he just sat. She didn't have time or the inclination to wonder why. 'It was just a blessing', she thought. Sometimes he and his step-brother would sit close together, probably for comfort.

The baby girl didn't thrive. In the months ahead she developed croup and died a few days before her first birthday. Within three months Ollie was pregnant again. She was still mourning her baby girl. Hopefully this new life she was carrying gave her some comfort. She gave birth to another son who was named for her husband. She now had boys aged six and five at home with her newborn.

When David started school it gave Ollie a small amount of relief and it would have given David some, too. Maybe even Beulah and Edgar could visit if some kind soul would bring them by. 'It's possible that my husband will do that,' she thought. Some reason was wrought. She was given a year to recover before becoming pregnant again and he did take her to visit her children.

It was about this time in the early 1920's that the newspapers began writing about trouble in the mills. After the war, the need for fabric started to slow down. The mills began cutting the number of employees and expecting more from those they kept on.

The orphanage notified Ollie that a husband and wife wanted to adopt Beulah; a couple that would see that she had a secure life until she was ready to marry. They made plain they would keep Ollie in their lives and they kept their word. That Ollie agreed to this plan was a big leap of faith for her but also gave a window into her current life. I believe she wanted to make sure one of her children had a safe life.

She gave birth to two girls and another boy. David was handy around the house and learned to diaper the babies when Ollie was called to another need.

Lewis, Garland, David

Thelma, Wade, Louise

David had asthma as a child. He became stronger and fended it off better after he started school but it would start up often enough. It was hard to sleep at home; there was always a child sick or hurt in this house. David also walked in his sleep. He was usually awakened before he left the house since someone was always awake. No, he didn't get enough sleep during this happy time when he was allowed to go to school.

When the three boys were in school, she now had two toddlers and a baby to tend, again. Her husband was spending less time at home these days. But since he was a good provider, she didn't complain much. Actually she didn't have much time to think about it. She did know that a lot of men were out of work now.

And the mills and their workers were at loggerheads. Workers started walking out on strike as close as Marion and Gastonia. They wanted more rights as workers like northern mill workers were getting. Being from Gaston County, Ollie was worried about friends and family that still lived and worked there. Newspapers told about confrontations between police and the strikers; and that some who were familiar with the mills thought the police would be loyal to the owners since they sometimes paid their salary. When people read about strikers being shot down in a southern state more of them changed their minds about striking.

Ollie began to worry that this trouble might come here. It was well known the mills were owned by northerners, drawn to this town because of some fellow Italians from northwest Italy, Waldensians, who had settled here in the latter part of the nineteenth century. She wondered if this would make a difference in how their workers reacted to the news of strikes in surrounding areas. She also worried about the children who were in school. It was close by some of the mills.

David liked school. He was quiet and paid attention to his teachers. They made him feel special, giving him attention that he didn't receive at home. This made him try harder to excel. He listened to stories and began to read about the early history of his country. He saw maps of the world with all the oceans. For the first time in his life he began to see a future - his future. It was likely here he began thinking that a man's life seemed to begin only when he could escape domestic life.

He learned that he was good with his hands. A ball fit perfectly and was guided by his brain to the best advantage. He held a hammer with assurance, building tables and other projects for his teachers. The problem was getting enough rest at night to enjoy his school days. He had chores at home, hopefully out of doors. Inside was pretty much chaos as problems with his mama and her husband became worse.

David enjoyed school but when he had just turned sixteen Ollie told him she needed him to leave school and go to work. She didn't say that the family wasn't getting support from her husband but David figured it out. He asked him one night when he walked in the door after being gone for most of the week. His step-father raised his arm to hit him but found himself on the floor instead. From that time on they avoided each other. And David went to work at the mill.

Then the whole country fell into depression. Mills were closing all around.

When David lost his job the family had to depend on their garden and what Ollie had managed to put by. Their whole world was in a state of flux again. A couple of neighborhood boys and David decided to try for a job where people were getting ready for the World's Fair in Chicago. Without telling their folks of their plans they had learned which freight train to catch to start them in the right direction.

The boys managed to meet up with men who were also headed for Chicago who knew how to scavenge food and survived to tell the tale. At night when David sometimes walked in his sleep, someone must have been awake to keep him from falling out of a moving train or wandering away from safety. The campfires with so many men trying to find food and keep warm was a dangerous place for the boys. They stopped at a farmhouse one early morning, hoping to do odd jobs in exchange for food. They could see the lady of the house peering through her window when they knocked on her door but she never opened it. She turned away, disappearing from sight as they heard a baby start to cry from somewhere in the house. She was afraid of them. They looked a motley bunch.

They started back home without finding work. They wouldn't forget this experience and often wondered how they had managed to keep safe and return to their parents.

Valdese friends, back in the day.

From left Zinnie Canipe, unknown, Mr. Brown ("Brownie,") unknown, unknown, David Turner, end right, 1930's

CHAPTER 3

"*You probably need some water, David. Maybe you should get back in bed, too.*" *The doctor watched as David sat on his bed, but didn't remove his slippers. He still sat erect as if at attention.*

"*Now, I see you have a wife and two children at home.*"

"*Sir! Yes Sir. They are sharing a house with my half-brother and his wife. He was given a medical discharge, too, after he was drafted. Edith is working; she has someone in to watch the kids.*" *David lay back, trying to relax.*

"*Well, now. I see that you volunteered for service. What did your wife think of that?*"

David ducked his head. "*She didn't know, Sir. Not until I was in Charlotte, waiting to be sworn; that's North Carolina, Sir. I had to send her a telegram then, asking for a sworn affidavit; that it was alright with her.*"

"*You didn't know that married men with children couldn't just enlist, then? Is there a reason you didn't talk about this decision with your wife?*"

A look of puzzlement came over David's face. "*I wonder why often enough. I think I hoped to see the world, Sir, while providing for my family.*" *He shook his head.* "*No, looking back, I was only thinking of seeing the world. I hoped to support my family, too.*"

He didn't mention the baseball player who came to town in 1937, the one who David met at the recreation center and watched play baseball.

"I see you've had a furlough home and Mrs. Turner has visited you here. You know you're being discharged because of your health. Will you take up your responsibilities at home with your wife and children?"

David's hands trembled as he plucked at his sheet. "Sir, I doubt I have been a good husband or father so far. I hope I can now, with the help of God."

His mind went back to a small creek, the icy water coming down from the South Mountains, where he was baptized at about age 12. He was also thinking about the chaplain who had invited him to attend services at a local church here. He had made his peace there after asking forgiveness for his many transgressions. David wanted to be a better man. He didn't know his chaplain had written Edith a letter saying he believed David had changed and would be a good husband to her.

—⊶⊷—

Ellyson Field
US Naval Air Station
Pensacola, Florida   *October 25, 1942*

Dear Mrs. Turner.

You will be happy to hear the good news about David. Following our worship service this morning he lingered to the last, saying he wanted to talk with me. He confessed to the way he has treated you; of the sorrow, heartaches, worry and trouble he has caused you. He spoke so highly of what a good wife you had been to him, of his fine children to whom he had been an unworthy father and husband.

After we talked we knelt and prayed. I wish you could have heard his prayer for forgiveness to God for his sins and his love for you and his children; his determination by God's help to live a Christian life, to be the man God wanted him to be.

He needs our faith in him. I know he is in earnest and I believe he will remain true to his new stand to live a Christian life.

Very sincerely yours,
Chaplain W. Keeler Lt. USNR

The doctor looked at his watch. "Why don't you tell me about your wife?" He looked down at his file. "Tell me about Edith."

David looked into space. "She is a pretty woman, Sir. Her parents and family care for her. They gave me a chance because she wanted me. Now. .," David lifted his hands.

(Telling Mother and Dad's story here takes me back to a special place.)

They were singing "Coming 'round the Mountain" as the car swayed around the curves. David looked out the window but closed his eyes when they found nothing; space dropped away.

"Boys, I don't know. Are you sure you know where you're going? Swallowing, he wondered if he was going to be carsick.

"You just wait, Dave, old boy. Wonders are at the top of this road." Dwayne shook his head and gripped Eddie's arm. He rolled his eyes and pointed as a small rock building came into sight.

"We're here. Just look at that."

Dwayne had met Ida McKinney and her friends a few weeks ago in Banner Elk where they had attended Lee's McRae Institute. The girls had come for a reunion of sorts with some of their friends where they had gone to school.

He learned she would be home this week and wanted to show his friends these classy ladies. He hoped he had made a good impression.

(It was a good thing these young men were coming up here to meet pretty girls. It was well known that there were places where they could also get home-made whiskey if they had the contacts and knew where to go. You better know, since you could easily take a load of buckshot if you didn't.)

There were a few houses on a hillside on the other side of the road across from the rock building. Unpaved roads, almost swallowed by hardwood trees, forked off disappearing from sight. A light wind, spiced with strange, unknown smells came through the lowered windows of the car.

A young woman came out of the building with a packet of letters in her hand. Noting a sign, U. S. Post Office, Little Switzerland, N. C., on the window, David thought she must have been to pick up her family's mail.

She had brown, almost auburn hair, dark brown eyes, and a deep dimple in each cheek. She was also an innocent in that year, 1934.

Dwayne stopped the car along beside her. "Hey, pretty girl. I wonder if you can help me out."

She turned, pausing beside the open window. "Edith is my name and maybe I can."

David was struck dumb as he heard Dwayne ask, "Do you know where I can find Ida McKinney?" This was the prettiest girl he had seen in his lifetime.

Edith's eyes sparkled as she smiled. "She's my sister. Just follow this road and take the second road to your right. It's the first house you come to."

Dwayne said, "Thank you kindly, and may I offer you a ride home?" His mouth fell open when he saw her open the back door, watched David slide over, and Edith sit beside him.

(These young men didn't know that Edith felt she was in competition with her older sisters; that she was ready to compete with them. Of course you never know about another person's feelings. You might think you do, but you don't. Her sisters thought of Edith as 'impetuous,' jumping into a situation before thinking what she would do if she might change her mind. What David saw was a young woman who seemed newly minted like a shiny coin. Neither were thinking of a world that might tarnish her bright spirit.)

The McKinney Sisters, 1934: Back, Edith; front left Thelma, Missouri and Ida.

As they turned onto a deeply rutted road at the second turn-off, Dwayne was careful to steer the car so the tires straddled them. It was a good thing the road was dry. They passed pastures on one side and a fenced kitchen garden on the other. Coming past grape vines upon a small hill, Edith had directed them to a parking spot. A line of young White Pines lined the road almost hiding the house. Looking in the mirror Dwayne saw Edith taking her hand from David's. They had been holding hands.

David had gently taken the hand she had on the seat between them. The gesture was almost protective and her hand just automatically curled around his.

Edith's sisters, Ida, Thelma, and Missouri (Missouri was named by their grandmother, Nancy Buchanan,) were sitting on the porch waiting for the mail when the car pulled up. They didn't know what to make of Edith getting out of the car with three strangers. Edith passed letters to each, keeping her own. The number each received may indicate their popularity with young men but it also showed how good they were getting each to think they were the one and only.

A middle aged man the young men learned was the girls' father, Fons McKinney, walked out the door as Edith sat down on the steps. They had noticed an elderly woman sitting in a chair beside a window looking out as they walked by. David figured she was their granny. Then Ida recognized Dwayne. She introduced their dad to him, and Dwayne introduced Eddie and David to him. Satisfied they wouldn't be leaving the premises, Mr. McKinney went back in the house.

"Where are your friends?" Dwayne looked at the beautiful McKinney sisters with an impish grin.

"These are my sisters, Thelma and Missouri. Looks like you've met Edith. My 'friends' are going about their own business today. Now, who are your friends?"

"David is a 'traveling man' who has been all the way to Chicago to the World's Fair." Dwayne didn't bother to say that the fair hadn't opened yet when he was there.

Eddie became a bold adventurer, too. "Eddie here likes to take a canoe out on the Catawba River looking for sunken treasure close by where the ferries used to travel."

Missouri directed her attention to Dwayne and they walked down the steps to continue their conversation out in the front yard. Eddie's face went from pink to bright red as he said hello to each sister. He didn't know how to proceed with this bevy of pretty girls. He knew they had more than one boyfriend judging by their letters and the competition for their attention would be a contest of wills; then Ida told him she had a special boyfriend.

Eddie asked what they did for fun around here. "Do you have dances or anything?"

He soon found out that this was a popular pastime here as well as down the mountain. Ida told him about the young men who came from close by towns to claim a dance from Thelma. It seemed she was a sought after partner and was becoming the 'belle of every ball' with her dancing skills.

They learned these girls weren't country bumpkins, so to speak. Ida and Thelma still returned to their school to socialize with friends and visit special places in Banner Elk although they graduated a few years before. They had lived in a dormitory with young women from families of varied backgrounds at Lee's McRae Institute; some well-to-do, educated, and wily as some young girls are likely to be. Learning to make their way around this new environment would stand them well in their future. Missouri was brought into their world but Edith was still an outsider when she met David.

David sat down beside Edith on the steps. He felt important and proud that she gave her attention to him that day. She took his breath when she stood close to him and even took his hand when they said goodbye. He couldn't help himself when he leaned close and whispered that he would see her soon.

———————

He managed trips up the mountain with Dwayne as the months went by. Eddie had lost out this time. Sometimes Missouri made up a foursome but usually he had to look elsewhere. Missouri was a popular girl. Thelma kept her distance from what she thought as 'those town boys.' She made her feelings known to her sisters.

The winter months brought plenty of snow to this place. When the wind was blowing through the pine trees, making it even colder, the McKinney family was housebound and visitors were few and far between. Fons sometimes needed to shovel a path all the way to the barn to care for the cow but the poor chickens mostly became a meal. Letters were written before the fireplace, though, and someone would be coming by from time to time and take them to be mailed and returning with a stack for the sisters. (Some years later I would read the sister's letters on cold rainy days while visiting my grandparents. I remember they were kept in a tall cardboard box.)

Jane, their mother, kept up a correspondence with friends (Ida and Harry Hand) who lived in Florida most of the winter.

Their daughter, Harriet, had gone to Lee's McRae with Ida for high school, too, and spent many of the school's winter holidays with the family.

David had noticed the ways of this family that operated like one from a story book to him. Jane welcomed Fons as he came in the door. A good meal would be ready to be put on the table. After supper he would go about taking care of the animals while their daughters put away the food and cleaned the kitchen. Then everyone would talk about their day, laughing together or lamenting a sorrow in the area before talking about what would occupy them tomorrow.

He saw that Fons liked to listen to commentators talking about the latest news and the politics of the day on a battery-powered radio in the living room. He was an outspoken Republican in the area. He would get especially excited hearing about President Roosevelt trying to deal with the huge Depression sweeping the country. Fons was sure any Democrat was likely to make matters worse.

But the big news coming out of Raleigh was a big controversy about a new highway being planned by the Federal government; one that would come down through Virginia and across these very mountains. Fons knew his friend, Heriot Clarkson, was exerting pressure to have this place, Little Switzerland, have access on and off this highway. David was careful to keep his political thinking to himself.

After their father went to bed, the sisters told him, they would find dance tunes so they could practice their dance steps, making sure the volume was low. They dreaded the times their dad would come quietly into the room having been awakened. With his arms crossed and dressed only in his long drawers, he would send them off to bed, grumbling about their daughters using up the life of his radio's battery.

Although the nearest town had electricity, those living outside of town and in this community did not. It would be well over another ten years before lines carrying this precious commodity would be strung through this rugged terrain to connect people here to the outside world.

David was learning about Edith's family but some things weren't talked about.

Mary Jane Buchanan Snipes was a widow when she married Fons McKinney the 17th day of June. The year was 1910, a time for many changes here where her Mother and Dad had settled. Their place name changed to Little Switzerland. It was to be a summer colony founded by a lowland man named Heriot Clarkson. This is the story of how her family and the Clarkson family became connected.

To start, Jane's mother was a Deweese, named Nancy Melissa. Nancy's mother was Rachel McKinney, daughter of old Charlie McKinney, her great grandpa. Granny Rachel is the one who traveled to St. Louie with her husband, Louis Deweese, way back in 1830. He died there and Rachel brought her family back to her North Carolina home.

Nancy married William A. Buchanan. They had six boys and three girls. They all played a part in how this place came about (except the two boys who died as babies.) One son in particular wove the thread that bound them, though he was already gone from them. His name was Joseph (Joe) Neal Buchanan, Jane's youngest brother.

Joe was given the duty to care for Nancy and his invalid sister, Lula, by William. He said this in his Last Will and Testament, as he expected to die from his war wounds before reaching old age. He soldiered for the Confederacy, mostly in Virginia. He made sure to leave all of his farm and other earthly goods to Nancy except some land in McDowell County to Jane, Joe, and John Henry. He did make plain that Joe would receive the farm and home place upon Nancy's death. William died in 1903, the year Joe married. Sad to say but Joe fell from a high trestle while working for the railroad, down in a place called Bostic Junction. He died that day, December 16, 1908. Fons McKinney was coming to call on Jane by then. He had told Nancy that he wanted her as his wife.

When Heriot Clarkson started buying up land he wanted Jane's brother's and Nancy's land, too. His representative bought Nancy's from her son's widow, but Nancy Deweese Buchanan had her Dower Rights until her death. The Switzerland Company owned it but couldn't use it until she died. Going back to 1910, Fons and Jane rented their first house from The Switzerland Company. Actually, Fons was raised in this house and maybe, his mother before him. It's funny how it became a home to many generations before coming to them through a summer colony.

Fons McKinney, left, back row, seated.

Fons was a handy carpenter. Early on he and Mr. Clarkson (who later became Judge Clarkson) grew to know each other and both liked what they saw. A mutual respect matured into a lasting friendship. Soon Fons was helping build a lodge, along with his kin and neighbors. From that beginning he was singled out to contract and build homes for some of the incoming summer residents. As Mr. Clarkson relayed, "Fons could be trusted to work with their architects and put forth a structure from their printed lines."

During their first year of marriage, Mr. Clarkson's sister, Ida Clarkson Jones, and Jane came to know each other. Their house was close by and the lodge was built near the family cemetery, where Nancy and Jane visited regularly. Mrs. Jones acted as proprietor. She presided over a bountiful table for her lodgers. Much of the bounty on her table came from the gardens of the locals. It was a pleasure for Jane to visit her. They were of an age and commonality that their different cultures brought them to friendship. Fons and Jane were expecting their first child. Ida and Jane talked many a day while she picked through her raspberries or stripped early peas from their pods. When their daughter was born, Jane named her Ida Jones McKinney. I imagine a lot of folks wondered about that and maybe still do. As the years went by, all of Jane's daughters loved Ida. This friendship was another thread lending strength to the tapestry of their connection.

And Nancy was yet another one. Her husband, William A. Buchanan, was a teacher, soldier, and a right smart man. He took good care of his family, keeping the price of hogs, corn, and goods for his advantage in farming. He also bought up good pieces of land for his children and to keep. So when Nancy met the Clarkson family there must have been information passed about earning interest on money invested. However it happened, Nancy began sending money, through Ida Clarkson Jones, to a company in Charlotte. She must have earned good money since there was never a complaint from her. We have the respectful letters sent to her by the owner, always giving his respects to her and family.

Lawrence, Jane, Ida and Fons McKinney, 1911

When Heriot Clarkson wrote his contract for the future of Little Switzerland, he made a covenant with Nancy Deweese Buchanan. He was to see that her family cemetery would remain, undisturbed, intact, in perpetuity. Each year on Decoration Day, flowers were placed on the well-tended graves, a preacher brought his message of resurrection, and songs were lifted up. Yet it is told that he, Mr. Clarkson, fully believed that someday the cemetery could be moved. As the years went by, as each Decoration Day came, Nancy was brought to preside over the proceedings. I believe that her dignity and care won him over, but then again, he may have seen her strength and determination and he thought better of crossing this woman. Whatever the reason, the threads of this family friendship held and the cemetery is there to this day.

Buchanan Cemetery beside Switzerland Inn, Little Switzerland

David learned there was plenty of hard work for everyone except their granny, Nancy Buchanan. She had done her work in the years past and was content to dream about those days now that she was in her 90's.

But it was during this time she dictated her life story to Jane which had begun almost 100 years before. She told about her parents homesteading in Missouri and her mother bringing her and her sisters back to North Carolina after their father died there. Nancy had named several of her granddaughters,

Missouri, in honor of this trip. Edith's sister was one of them. Her granddaughters were in awe of her when she told of 'hiring' herself out to a neighbor after her mother remarried, working long hours in his fields in the summer and helping his wife in the house in the winter. She was able to bring her own 'dowry' when she married in 1860 which was a big help in setting up a home during this turbulent time. Then the country split and war was declared. It would bring tragedy to this young couple.

The McKinney sisters considered Nancy Buchanan's show of independence in the late 1850's a rarity of the times since young girls were kept closer now. They would find in their own lives that personal circumstance and economics of the time could always start a different culture and family life.

CHAPTER 4

But it was a family life like Fons and Jane had that David longed for. This is about the time talk of a secret wedding began.

He told Dwayne, "Edith is a 'good' girl. I can't do what I want and just walk away. A man has to respect someone like her."

The pride of having such a beauty for his wife played a part, too. Edith had told him in private about going to the O'Henry Hotel in Greensboro to represent her town in the Miss North Carolina contest earlier in the year they had met.

It's a wonder she agreed to get married. No one knew then that Ida was so in love with a young man that they thought they had to marry. She was the first to have a secret wedding though and this may have given Edith (and David) courage to go forward.

Edith had her doubts, though. 'I wonder what married life will be like?' she thought. 'I know Mama and Dad have worked hard to make a good life for us daughters. I don't know if David, well either of us, can live up to them.'

He had male friends who enjoyed flashy clothes and being young men about town. Yes, Thelma had picked up on this pretty quick. They had ideas as to what their role was in the scheme of things: women were to be enjoyed, taught their place, and the world was theirs. David had learned their ways quickly. A railroad crew would have put up a caution flare on Edith and David's union.

And like most men, David would have the puzzle of figuring out the difference between this pretty girl and her role as his wife. No doubt he didn't think much about his role; working to take care of her and their children when they came along. With David leaving school early to help support his mother, Ollie, and her second family, he would be limited in his choice of jobs.

David told Ollie of the upcoming wedding and she was helping him find a place to bring his bride and get some furnishings together. She felt she owed him, I think. There were few places other than sharing a house. There might be a room or two above a store in town.

She wondered what David and Edith were thinking. They were walking down the street in Valdese looking in the window of a furniture store when she took his arm.

"David, you are so young, too young to realize what may happen as time goes by. I know you want to get away, out on your own. But marriage will bring children. Have you thought of that?"

Shaking his head no, he stopped walking. "Mama, I don't think it's right bringing children into this world. It will be awhile before I can think different about that." He began to walk again.

"David, in a marriage there is no way you cannot have children unless you are barren. If there was a sure way most women wouldn't continue to have them until they can no longer conceive. Please think on that."

He shook his head thinking he knew how even if his mother didn't and they walked on. He knew well about his step-father and his mother's difficult years raising her second family. He was glad now that his brothers were older and could help support the family.

His sister, Beulah, had gone to Nursing School after graduating from high school. Ollie was happy that she had grown up in a loving family and was doing well. Beulah stayed close to her mother, keeping up with her brothers, and half-brothers and half-sisters as best she could.

Since Ollie had filed for divorce recently the family didn't see much of their dad anymore. Divorce was rare in this time but she felt it was necessary in her case. He was a faithless husband who didn't take care of his family.

Little did a nineteen year old know that marrying didn't loosen the bonds of responsibility, not a little bit. His mother had tried to tell him and she did try to talk David out of it. Ollie remembered too well when her husband died, leaving her with three young children. She felt she had to put Beulah and Edgar in an orphan's home. Well, they were better off than David, that's for sure.

Edith was careful to keep her activities close to her routine. She wanted to keep the news of her coming marriage to David from her dad since she knew he wouldn't allow it. They slipped away in the spring of 1935 when the leaves on the hardwoods opened to shades of green and a gentle red.

David was nervous when he picked her up that day. His eyes widened when he saw her in a dress of palest yellow. "You look beautiful, Edith." His voice cracked as he said this while handing her into the car.

"Do you think we can get married and get me back home so Dad won't be suspicious, David?"

"I told Mama and Dad that your mother invited me to dinner, the reason you were picking me up so early, but we would be back before dark." She remembered her parents looking at each other with a solemn expression.

"The minister and his wife will be ready for us. I just wish we could be together instead of waiting for a place of our own, but I sure can't bring you to Mama's house."

"And our house is full to bursting. We can wait, David. I need to finish school."

David started the car, knowing they had no choice but to wait. He had arranged for a minister to marry them at the parsonage in a small community near his hometown about 12:00 noon. As they said their vows one phrase stuck in his mind, 'until death do us part.' These words would come back to haunt him in their future years together.

He dutifully returned Edith to her mountain home where she stayed, waiting for her husband to ready their home.

———— ∞ ————

Being the youngest of an extended family, Edith was just beginning to find her way in the family and this community. Like her sisters, she had grown up with her 'summer' friends and her cousins who lived close by. Finding her place with these older sisters has proved difficult, however.

When they grew up they became a unit putting Edith, the youngest, in the position as a tag along. In trying to gain their attention, she instead became a pest or so they thought. She never discussed this time of not feeling included with anyone but her sisters; you only knew how much she loved them. Being a pretty girl in her own right she soon had plenty of young men paying her attention.

This changed her family status some with her sisters. After all, Fons and Jane wouldn't allow her to date without chaperons or a group which included them. Then she was singled out, winning a beauty contest. She would represent the town where she went to school in the Miss North Carolina pageant to be held in Greensboro. Missouri was first runner-up. Edith was seventeen.

This was a time that she had needed her sisters and her parents. Thelma, Ida and Missouri hadn't been much help. At least Fons and Jane were there although they were worried that she was too young for such a responsibility. Now, at age eighteen, she has a husband.

Keeping her marriage a secret wasn't easy. She had to turn away former boyfriends, making various excuses. One day a young man from Morganton, N. C. knocked on the door asking for her.

"Edith, do you have a date today?" He shuffled his feet some but gave her a bright smile.

In a piquing mood she said, "No, but I have a husband."

He caused quite a commotion when he blurted out "Married? When did you get married?" The jig was up then. Maybe now her sisters would let her in the kitchen. She still needed to learn to cook.

On the day the news of Edith's marriage came out, Ida asked if she would walk with her to their grandmother's house to pick early apples. It was standing empty now that she lived with the McKinney's. Thelma and Missouri were helping Jane make a pattern for a dress they were showing her in a magazine. They were trying to occupy their minds but all of the sisters knew their Dad would be home soon and Edith would have to face him.

In early June there was softness to the air; insects sang while roaming chickens pecked here and there amongst the dirt and tuffs of grass. Their dad had replaced the ones they ate during the winter and the sitting hens now had little dibbies.

Ida and Edith walked past the henhouse where the chickens went to roost. Fons would be shutting the henhouse door in the early evening; this protected them from foxes. His chickens knew what to expect.

"Lord, Edith. Are you sure you want to leave school? You're so young to leave home and, and Dad is going to be mad as a wet hen."

She had chickens on her mind alright.

"He will be, and I dread it. Mama looked so sad I had to get out of there. Ida, I don't know what I was thinking. I'm so tired of being just a pest to be pushed aside. I'm a woman, too, and I wanted you and Missouri and Thelma to know that. Being the youngest isn't easy when your sisters don't take you seriously."

Tears began sliding down Edith's cheeks. "When I knew you had slipped away to marry Gaylord, it gave me courage to say yes to David. I was right surprised when he asked me, though. I think he was, too. Now I'm beginning to have second thoughts."

Ida took Edith's arm after wiping her tears with her hand. She took a deep breath. "Edith, you know I'm going to keep quiet about my marriage to Gaylord. I want to finish out the year here teaching school but then I'll be with him."

Ida was teaching a class in their small wooden church within walking distance of their home. Her class was made up of children of various ages in this small community. At this time, a woman couldn't teach school if she was married.

They began putting apples in their sack and then started walking a path crowded by mountain laurels on each side. They

41

would be in full bloom soon. Edith took note of all that was familiar and knew she would be leaving a place she loved.

Ida stopped and put down her side of the sack of apples. Taking Edith's hand, she squeezed it before letting go.

"I'm sorry we weren't more help when you were getting ready to go to the pageant. Maybe we thought Dad wouldn't let you go. You're right that we didn't realize you are grown up now. I hope we can make amends."

Edith swallowed past a lump in her throat.

Their Dad opened the door for them when they walked up on the porch. Taking the apples, he looked at Edith. "We need to talk, young lady." He sat the apples by the door and took her arm, walking her back outside. It was a nice warm day and he indicated they were to sit on the steps. He looked at Edith, just waiting.

Edith swallowed. "Dad, I may have made a mistake." Silence stretched like elastic waiting to be tacked on new bloomers.

"I liked David from the start and I thought, well, I wanted to be grown-up, too, so I married him."

She ducked her head as tears started a trail down her face again. Glancing up she saw a look of pain on her Dad's face.

He wouldn't know yet that this pain of being unable to protect his child might go on, even until death.

"Edith, I wanted to keep you at home for me and your mama. Just for a while, you see, just for a while." He turned away, his blue eyes almost sparkling, like tears were forming.

Looking around Fons saw his vines that would be heavy with blue grapes soon; his garden had maturing fruits and vegetables. 'So much plenty,' he thought, 'and so many going hungry across our country.'

CHAPTER 5

Fons' way of life was one that his family had known for generations here. But his daughters were no longer just mountain girls. No, the ways of the outside world had invaded his home years ago. The people who came here had brought opportunity and jobs; they also brought new ideas and cultures. Well, some things were new but not everything.

Fons found that this well-to-do group did not all think alike; some were Republicans, like him, but some were Democrats. In fact a good portion of them were Democrats, the opposite of most people already living in this part of the state. They had one thing in common though. The Negro community should be separate and know their place in the scheme of things. The new people brought them along to work as domestics in their homes and as time went on, in their business endeavors. This would go against the grain of those who still approved of the forced evacuation of all 'coloreds' in this county some years back.

The story had it that a Negro man had 'taken advantage' of a white woman and was escaping justice. All Negro families in the area were put them on a train. They left with instructions to never come back.

It was strange that so many mountain families clung to the party of Lincoln while disavowing the rights of Negroes.

Fons and others found working for these new people advantageous so a give and take became the norm. Soon their families were friends and their children were growing up together. His daughters, including Edith, didn't lack for suitors here. He knew it wasn't long ago when her favorite was a young man who played the guitar and sang to her under a full moon.

He sometimes overheard his daughters talking but he never let on. That time it brought memories to him of Jane strolling with him under a night sky glowing with stars in April of 1910, then seeing a comet streak across; the night he proposed marriage.

What he didn't know was the reason Edith suffered a broken heart and they stopped seeing each other. As was usually the case, the young man saw older, more willing girls to satisfy his carnal needs. He contracted a venereal disease and gently told Edith he was leaving town because of his job (she learned the true story later).

Venereal disease was rampant in this time period as it was during the 19th Century. A woman was most fortunate if she didn't contract one of many diseases on her wedding night; her husband wouldn't know he had it most likely. Some could be passed on to their children at birth, too.

Fons tried to protect his daughters by setting up firm rules of conduct. Edith was chosen to represent Spruce Pine, where she went to high school, in the Miss North Carolina contest organized by the American Legion in 1934. Fons felt she was too young to stay in a big hotel with strangers. Two male chaperones from the school board went along and they assured him that Edith would be well protected. He had served on the board with them and trusted them to protect his daughter.

Edith had a grand time rehearsing and meeting the other contestants. What Fons didn't know was in spite of the rules set up to protect the girls, young men had made it to their room. Edith's roommate was from Salisbury, and she was chosen Miss North Carolina that year of 1934.

As Edith told the story, they knocked on their door just to see if the girls would open it. Of course they did but the young men took no for an answer when they asked to come in. It probably helped when they saw the house detective striding towards them.

It continued to amaze Fons that his youngest daughter, a child that liked to play pranks and tease her older sisters, had been picked as the prettiest one in her school.

Although his daughters had grown up with city families coming to their home, his and Jane's mothers and the extended families lived close by. They held their local customs, too. Fons thought of his own father who had died almost ten years ago. He always thought the loss of his grist mill in the big flood had taken his spirit right out of him although he lived almost another decade. It was hard to believe this vital man was gone, still. His mother was ill now and the local doctor couldn't seem to find out the cause. The family was hopeful she would recover soon.

She had cancer; tiny cells gone awry, eroding healthy cells in her body. Not a commonly known word or ailment at this time but one that would envelope many in the years to come. No one suspected when you disturbed these mountains by mining the valuable minerals, toxic materials could be unleashed, becoming part of the ground water, fresh water springs, and wells. Others in this family who grew up close by this mining would fall ill with the same disease; Fons, the eldest son, and later one of his younger brothers was known to have cancer and would die from this disease. Three people in one family dying this way would cause one to be suspect of their environment in the future.

But as the daughters grew up the bonds of the 'summer' people tightened. Fons knew his daughters wouldn't be satisfied with the culture they were born into. The fact that they were smart and pretty opened doors that could and would cause trouble in any place or time. Young, healthy, pretty girls were always chosen for attention in any place. They easily slipped into this new society and welcomed the attention of young men who might offer them a different life.

Missouri had been keeping company with a young college student, the son of an attorney who was one of the original settlers of the summer colony set up in the midst of this mountain culture. His mother made the remark that she didn't want her son getting mixed up with a mountain girl. Missouri was the one to break off this relationship when she met another young college student she would later marry.

There's a sad part to this story. Missouri couldn't bring herself to tell the young man she had met someone else, someone she had fallen in love with and planned to marry; so he was the last to know. The memory of Missouri stayed with him through the years.

Fons' eldest daughter, Ida, had gone away to Banner Elk to a school that would help her prepare for college should she be able to go. When she graduated she took special teacher training and was teaching in a local school near her home. Thelma followed, learning to assist in a business office. To Fons, Thelma seemed the most sensible about the young men in this community. She was popular and enjoyed going out but didn't take them as seriously as his other daughters.

Above, Ida, and friends

He was glad his two older daughters had the opportunity to go to Lee's McRae. Jane's daughter, Effie, his stepdaughter, was now married and had a family of her own but she had been sent there first to attend school. She didn't like boarding, though and insisted on coming home. His youngest, Missouri and Edith, would choose another path.

He brought his mind back to his youngest daughter. "I like the looks of David, but he's young, about the same age I was when I married Lawrence's mother."

He remembers his wife lying there with a pool of blood spreading out, soaking their bed, leaving her infant son, young Lawrence, and Fons as she stopped breathing. Their infant had only survived a few months.

He looked at Edith. "Mistakes don't come into it. You made a promise to him and you must keep it. You're a married woman now so have him come for you."

"But . ., we haven't lived together, Dad. I thought to finish school here before going."

Edith, maybe, had hoped he would make this marriage go away. Her hopes were dashed with his next words.

Shaking his head, he stood and waited for her to stand. "We'll go in and tell your mother. She'll help you pack your clothes. You must write David to come for his wife."

Jane and Fons McKinney were both widowed with a child each when they married in 1910, the same year Ollie and June Turner married. It makes you wonder that they had watched the same comet in April of that year; that it possibly could have portended their fate, communicated with them and both couples had decided to marry.

These people would all come to feel a harmony with these tall mountains that surrounded their home place. Somehow David may have been connecting to the people who lived here because of them. Was the dust from these mountains part of the deep space where all dust returns, where all life comes from; part of a story we don't know yet?

Jane's mother, Nancy, disapproved when she and Fons decided to marry. She thought Jane should take her time choosing a husband, seeing her as a well to do widow with choices. What she hadn't known was that Jane felt her destiny was with Fons; that she didn't have a choice in the matter.

Jane wished she had reminded him of that time before telling him about Edith's marriage. 'No need,' she was thinking, as she saw him walk into the room. She could see the memories traveling across his face.

She wondered if Fons knew about the story Effie was spreading about his first wife's death; that he had knocked her off a fence where she was sitting soon after their son was born, causing her to bleed to death.

Jane's daughter from her first marriage still resented her stepdad and caused him trouble when she could. She could imagine her retelling the story she had heard about Hattie falling off a fence and saying to her audience, 'well, he probably knocked her off,' or maybe that's how she heard the story. Knowing Effie as her mother did, Jane thought she liked that ending and told it where she could cause the most trouble. Lord, she hoped Fons never found out what she was doing. (And his daughters better not find out either. Their dad could do no wrong in their eyes.)

Jane looked at her mother sitting in her rocker before the fire. It warmed her old bones and gave warmth to the chilly evenings, necessary even in the summer here in the mountains.

She would have lots to tell her when they were alone. Nancy could no longer do for herself and couldn't be left alone. She was hard of hearing so missed a lot of conversations. She didn't miss the expressions on her family's faces though and Jane knew she would expect the full story.

Jane was lonely now that her daughters were grown up and out of the house a lot. She remembers the many family activities when she and Fons were with them; picnics and cookouts were special times. She would miss Edith as Nancy would miss her granddaughter, too. Edith was the one that reminded Nancy most of herself.

Edith, 1934-35

CHAPTER 6

Nancy still talked about her experiences during the War Between the States. Her husband, William Buchanan, fought with the 22nd Regiment North Carolina Troops, part of Lee's Northern Army of Virginia. Although he was wounded, he survived the war and returned to Nancy and their family; but he was no longer the strong, healthy man she had married. He was a teacher before the war so he returned to this occupation. Their future would continue to be filled with tragedies.

Two of their young sons died within days of each other in 1874 from diphtheria and in 1898, the year Jane and Vance Snipes married, they lost their eldest son to consumption. Yet they were together and could support each other during their losses. In the year of 1903, however, and through the end of that decade, personal tragedies brought Nancy to her knees.

1903 started with the joyful occasion of their youngest son's marriage but in just two weeks their youngest daughter died of pneumonia. She was weakened by complications from a childhood case of meningitis; three months later Nancy's husband died and then their widowed daughter-in-law passed away with consumption, some five years after her husband, leaving young children to be cared for. In 1904 Nancy's mother passed away.

Nancy brought two of her orphaned granddaughters to live with her and her youngest son, his wife and their two daughters. We don't know how it came to be but the youngest child suffered traumas here with Nancy that always plagued her relationship with her grandmother.

In 1908 this youngest son died in a horrible accident and then his brother, only 35 years old, passed away from a lingering wound he had received some years earlier. These men, too, left widows with young children. Of Nancy and William's nine children only three survived to live to old age.

In the same year of 1908, Jane's husband (Effie's father) passed away with Bright's disease. Then Jane, too, with her young daughter moved in with Nancy. There were now three widows and at different times from three to five young children living here. Nancy was 66 years old in 1908. She would die in 1935, at age 93. She carried on but without the support of her beloved husband.

During this time Nancy made investments with Charlotte, N. C. companies for the interest they paid. She was introduced to these people by her friends who started this mountain summer colony.

> Elba Manufacturing Co.
> Cotton Seed Oil, Meal, Hulls and Linters
> Mills at Charlotte, N. C. and Maxton, N. C.
> Head Office: Charlotte, N. C.
> T. J. Davis, President and Gen. Mgr.
>
> December 10, 1922
>
> Mrs. Nancy Buchanan
> Little Switzerland, NC

Dear Mrs. Buchanan:

I received a letter from Mrs. Ida C. Jones, enclosing check for $100.00, which she stated you wished her to turn over to me to be used in connection with other funds received from you.

I am handing you herewith our note for $100.00 which bears the same rate of interest that we have been paying you and interest will be credited on your several notes semi-annually, as has been our custom, and check mailed to cover amount due.

We are having very disagreeable weather, and it now looks like we will have snow in the next day or two.

Mrs. Davis and the children are as well as usual and join me in kind regards. (Signed T. J. Davis)

She also bought a car and her step-grandson, Lawrence, drove the family on their errands to the nearest town. This caused hard feelings with her eldest daughter since Nancy was living with Jane and Fons and their family at the time. She ended up selling the car and enjoyed visiting her three surviving children through these years.

Edith's maternal grandfather survived the war and sired most of their children after he came home. David's great-grandfather died in this same war; but he left three children, one of whom would become his grandfather, Ellis Leander Turner. Because of these circumstances Edith and David and their children came to be. But there's another patriarch in Edith's family who gave them life; one who was drawn to these ancient mountains, too. He is Fons' (and Jane's) great-grandfather, Charles McKinney.

Fons' family didn't talk about Charles. His daughters grew up not knowing their connection to him or his story.

———— ✖✖✖ ————

Charles McKinney came to these ancient mountains of the Blue Ridge sometime in the late 1700's and would leave many descendants. He is best known for his unusual lifestyle. This is most likely why Fons, Jane and Nancy don't mention him. There are many stories written about him; people trying to imagine what he was like. Here is one of them:

An Interview with Charles McKinney of McKinney Gap, by Out Yonder News, July 4, 1850

_____

"*My best days are gone but I lived. Yes, I lived.*"

The old man looked straight at me but his blue eyes peering beneath bushy brows were seeing another time. He began to move his old rocking chair back and forth, back and forth, as we sat together on the front porch of his cabin. His head swiveled, looking at the dark-blue mountains spread out before us.

"*I reckon I picked the right place to settle back then when this country was in turmoil. Little government back here, you know. We made the best of what was offered and tended to our business while living close by Indians; we settled our own affairs mostly.*"

"Well, Sir, I'm a reporter and your reputation for, uh, an unusual life style is getting outside your domain, so to speak. How do you reckon you came to these circumstances, Sir?"

He turned in his chair, looking north. "*Why, I was a young buck back when the new century was getting close. You had to make your own way somehow. I worked our farm there in southwest Virginny and hired myself out, finding jobs where I could. My pa allowed me to make my own crop once in a while so I might sell some, taking them around close-by settlements. I used my Pa's horse and wagon when it weren't needed at home. Of course drovers from Caroline brought news of mountain land going wasting. I heard all the tales they had, ways to travel if you had a wagon, all that you know."*

His eyes wandered then he directed them back to me. *"Pa died in the spring. My ma told me I'd need to seek our fortune now. Sister married and her husband moved in with us to tend the farm. Right then I worked off a whole load of some plantings: apple, plum, peach, and started south with the best pull horse and wagon. My saplings were bartered for supplies and even a few coins. All's well except the wagon road just petered out."*

"I had to get where I was going and I wouldn't know it until I saw it. I found a settlement near the start of them big, blue, mountains you see out thar. I sold my wagon and set out riding my horse, following what was an Indian trail come to find out. Frost was nipping my leather leggings now. I stuffed the soles with soft moss lined with leaves to protect my feet. One morning I woke up hearing a splash of water coming over some rocks near a close by spring. Walking over to it I threw some water over my face and let out a yelp when it touched me. Blinking some I looked out and saw it. I was here, where I knew I'd get to."

This man seemed to have forgotten I was there as he continued his story.

"I made my camp and spent some days exploring on foot. I was thinking about riding down the mountain to Morganton to find the courthouse but my good luck didn't hold. My horse was

left to shelter and nourish himself those days while I wandered. This cold day I returned to find him missing. I searched for several days but lost his tracks in a stream down a ravine. Was it an Indian? Whoever, he was smart and I was on foot."

"I decided it was too late in the season to try to walk out. I sheltered my fire, hunted my supper and fared well until snow came in. Then I sheltered as best I could. I survived by chopping trees in the daylight hours to keep warm while building a sturdy cabin. It's a wonder but I was young and able. By spring I was a true mountain man who would have scared my own mother. I knew this by seeing myself in the clear stream."

"Well, uh, how about your wife, wives, then. There's a lot of interest you must know."

He got up, braced by his knobbed cane. He stared out, seeing faces, beloved faces. Speaking in a low voice he said *"I married . . . Elizabeth was her name. She died of the fever after my boy was born. Then I just had him and our first born daughter, babies too young to be without a mother."* He turned and sat.

"My wife's sister, Margaret, came to care for them. I was deep in grief. Still I had to provide, live. My hunting trips began to take me further away from home; sometimes I stayed away for the night. I began to come up on people."

"The first was a lone woman. She ran to me like she knew who I was. Her eyes were wild and red from weeping. She had stayed alone for some weeks, waiting for her husband. I calmed her some, told her I would chop some wood for her fire so she could cook, keep warm. She just shook her head and began gathering up her few pitiful things."

"I'm going with you. I can't stay here no more."

"I took her. Another woman walked in with two children who looked to be starving not long after. Lord knows how long it had taken her but she found us. I didn't turn her away; I began to build shelters. This was a wild place and people fended off wild animals, maybe strangers who might take all you have. People began to stick together more for protection. I believe word got around we had a safe place."

"What about the children? Word has it they all belong to you."

The old man laughed out loud. *"Well you* <u>hear</u> *things. I sired children and had more under my protection, their mothers too."*

"The story is told they were your wives, concubines if you will."

Charles looked directly in my eyes and winked, *"Now some things are rightly private, don't you think."*

———⊗⊗⊗———

This story brings to mind one that few know about in this family Charles' and Elizabeth's first child, Rachel, married a young man, Lewis Deweese, who took her off to homestead in Missouri. They were the parents of Nancy Deweese Buchanan and her sisters. But he wasn't just any young man. He and his siblings were born of a well-known preacher of the time, Garrett Deweese, and his wife, Suzannah Palmer Deweese. He was so much loved people named their children after him. The Reverend Deweese and his wife came from a long line of devout religious men going back all the way to the group that came to our country with William Penn. These early Deweese and Palmers knew General George Washington and became part of the Revolution against George III of England. It's quite a story and well worth your time to investigate. (See Toe River Valley Heritage-North Carolina, Volume 1, Article 311, by Lloyd Richard Bailey, Sr., Copyright 1994. There is more extensive information on the DeWeese and Palmer families in a similar type Buncombe County, NC book that I found in a local library.)

CHAPTER 7

The weekend came fast while Edith was busy packing her clothes. Thinking of leaving her home she realized her mistake. All the while she had wanted to be included in her older sisters' lives, and now she had cut herself off from them. She wouldn't be invited to Florida by family friends or take part in what she thought as her sisters' more sophisticated activities.

Edith was used to dressing to impress her 'summer' friends. She and her sisters had seen pictures of the latest fashion since their friends had newspapers and magazines with pictures of what ladies were wearing. Jane would look at a picture of a frock, make a pattern, and sew an exact copy. But this was a new situation for Edith. She didn't know what to expect.

Her family, Edith's sisters especially, seemed distracted as the day came for her to leave. Memories of their time together were crowding into their minds. They were realizing that precious times pass and can never be retrieved. Nancy, Jane, and Fons knew this would only be the first of many such partings and would never get easier.

David managed to borrow a car for the weekend. He followed Edith into the house as if he was Daniel walking into the lion's den. Fons' face was grave as he shook his hand.

"Welcome to our family, Son. I expect you to care for Edith. She is close to our heart. Be sure to arrange for mail at your new home and Edith you write and tell us all about it."

Edith thought he was anxious about her living out of his area and he was having regrets about sending her off to a strange and unknown place. Actually he liked David but knew he couldn't guarantee that he would be a good husband to his daughter.

They all had special gifts for the young couple: Fons carried a box with home canned fruits, vegetables, jams and some potatoes and apples he had stored over the winter; the sisters had gift-wrapped their own hand embroidered pillow cases and hand towels that they carried to the car. Granny Nancy pressed a $5 bill into her hand. David, Edith and Jane carried her personal belongings and gifts from her friends.

After a tearful goodbye they got into his friend's car. The family watched them drive out of sight with hopeful but heavy hearts.

David drove down the mountain, praying the brakes wouldn't give way. He had the car in low gear but he had to use the brakes, too. As they drove along the now familiar road, Edith leaned forward, not wanting to miss anything. It seems she had forgotten her trepidation about going off with her new husband. To her it had become an adventure, at this point anyway.

"Tell me about our place, David. Do we have a stove? Don't laugh at me, but I don't know much about cooking."

"Yes, and Mama has bought a few groceries and made sure we have ice in the icebox. Maybe we can get by. She has given us a few pots and pans."

He didn't know too much about cooking either but he could get a meal if he had to. Growing up there were times when there was no one but him to feed himself and hungry children.

"What's an icebox?"

Edith's family, those who grew up in these high mountains, and the 'summer' people who had adopted some of their ways, kept milk, butter and what few foods that needed to be kept cold in a small wooden building sitting over a cold mountain spring. She took for granted they would have running water in this kitchen since her dad had piped water from their spring through a faucet in their sink.

David had to laugh. "It's a wooden cabinet that has a place for a large piece of ice. The ice sits on a bed of sawdust but it slowly melts and the water has to be caught in a pan and emptied and the ice has to be replaced. It's not like a cold spring that runs through a spring house. You put your milk on a shelf above the ice"

Of course, the ice house in town had stored ice frozen last winter; keeping ice wasn't easy. What the people in this town would have to have soon was one of the 'new, fangled Frigidaire's.' With the summer heat ice was too hard to keep.

What David didn't say was that he would be paying for the icebox, stove and other items for some time to come.

"Well, that sounds like a lot of work but I guess it's better than having to go outside to get a crock of milk, anyway."

"Yeah, it isn't easy for someone to carry that ice up a flight of stairs at our place either."

Before she knew it David was parking in front of a two story building on the main street of her new home, Valdese, close by a large rock building. David told her it was where he had gone to school and that a new high school was being built nearby. The street was newly paved and David said plans were already made to pave more streets. David opened the trunk of the car and picked up her suitcase and she reached in for some smaller parcels and they started for the stairs leading up to their door.

"The door at the top is locked. I aim to carry you across the threshold just like any newly married man when I open it."

He grinned at her and let her go up in front of him. He sat the suitcase aside, opened the door with his key, and swooped Edith into his arms. When he put Edith down in the room he turned her close to his body.

"Edith, this is our new home." His heart seemed to skip a beat as he kissed her.

Walking in the room while holding her hand, he pulled a string hanging from the ceiling, turning on a bare light bulb. It flooded the room with light. Edith gasped. No one had electricity where she lived.

David walked over to a curtain and pulled it aside, stepping back to show Edith a double bed beside a chest of drawers. "Edith, you can put your clothes in here. I don't have much so the bottom drawer is all I need."

She found a place for her clothes but kept two drawers for David. He checked the icebox and saw milk, eggs, and a package he hoped was bacon. He figured they could cook these items after he got a fire going in the stove but first he had to carry the rest of their belongings up the stairs.

They both went back down the stairs and finished emptying the car. A stack of wood was just outside at the top of the stairs, another important item needing to be carried up the stairs.

They wouldn't starve, especially now that they had all these canned fruits and vegetables with the ones right out of the garden.

He watched as Edith walked over to put a thick book on their table, a wedding present from Ethel Hakes, Elise Hakes' (Edith's close friend) mother. It was a cookbook. In the years to come it would be so well thumbed it would fall apart.

Edith looked around then walked to a closed door beside the stairs outside their room. She opened it and saw a porcelain seat and a small sink. 'Thank you, Lord,' she thought. 'We have an inside toilet.'

David noticed the opened door. "Now Edith I need to tell you our arrangement. This room here was used as storage for the store downstairs but the owner agreed to rent it out to me. This toilet will be used by them during the day but we can use it too and when the store closes, it is all ours at night. You'll notice there's a new lock installed on the inside. Be sure and lock the door when you are in there during store hours and we must try to be quick about our business, too. Hopefully this will work for them and us."

"Looks like I'll need to scrub the sink and this commode every time before we use it then, since this sink is where we'll get all our water to wash and to clean our dishes." She remembered being taught about germs in school. Edith wondered about the other people who would use it.

The newlyweds laughed as David finally got a fire going and tried together, to fry up bacon and eggs. It was a mess. Edith insisted on heating water in the kettle to pour into a small pan to clean the dishes, then enough to put in the bathroom sink after she scrubbed it out so they could wash up, too. She was thankful they had packed soft, cotton towels and washcloths that her mother told her she would need.

By the time they were ready for bed, David wondered if he had the strength to consummate their marriage. He knew he would need to take special care with Edith who was scared but excited, too. When he found it was hard work penetrating a virgin they both decided it would be best to try again, maybe in the morning. That worked. (This is yet another story Edith would relay to her children many years later.)

———— ❦ ————

In the days ahead, David took Edith shopping for the necessary items they would need in their new home: more soap for bathing, washing dishes and hand washing their clothes, shaving soap for him and extra toilet paper. He showed her the town as they walked along the main street.

"Who are these ladies dressed in long, dark dresses?" Edith wanted to know. "It seems too hot for these clothes, even the little white bonnets."

He told her the history of how it came to be. "It was told to me that a group of people near the French-Italian Alps in Italy settled the town at the end of the 19th. Century. These people you see are some of the original settlers. I heard the story about how they were practically pushed out of their homeland many years before because they were Protestants, called Waldensians, instead of Catholics as most were in that country."

They often met some of the original settlers dressed in their native clothes, still speaking the language they grew up with in Italy. Some of these people were shorter in statue with dark hair and eyes; they were so different from the taller, fair haired, blue eyed people she was used to. It was a strange place to her. But Edith had heard some history of Italians living close by her family.

Early in the 20th Century there were many Italians coming into New York City from southern Italy when they were hearing about all the jobs here. Some moved down to the mountains of North Carolina, where they were hired on to help lay tracks for the railroad that would be crossing these mountains. They thought this a better situation than staying in the Italian community growing up in New York City where there was unrest and growing crime.

Building railroad tracks across the mountains was dangerous work. These, formed millions of years ago, had seen volcanoes, earthquakes, crashing continents and were purported as some of the oldest in the world. It now seems possible that old rock formations have old memories and men might be drawn into these memories. These southern Italians coming here to work had lived close by Vesuvius; one that destroyed many people long ago. Maybe these ancient places were drawing them here. We now know more than a few of these men were killed and buried building this railroad.

These Italian immigrants must have thought the history of their old country and this new one was ironic; when Italy came together into mostly a united country right after the time of the American Civil War, where the United States had fought to decide whether to stay together or pull apart.

The very next day, after he got off work, David arranged for a box at the post office. Edith had a letter ready to mail so he was able to put their return address on the envelope, buy a stamp and send it on the way.

Edith's sister, Missouri, came down to visit the newlyweds in just a few weeks. David had fixed her a comfortable bed on the floor with beautiful quilts Jane had sent in the mail. She had Dwayne as her escort for a dance being held close by. She brought Edith a new pink suit that Jane had made for her. Looking back, this was the night Edith insisted that she conceived their first child; the night David realized that he was possessive of his beautiful wife.

The business underneath their apartment was having the dance. They had made a small dance floor on one end of the room in front of the musicians who were playing popular tunes when the couples came in. It was a hot night towards the end of July. The musicians, one with a saxophone and the other on a piano, were playing the ever popular "April in Paris" as couples came up onto the floor. Edith was remembering the words, 'I never knew the charm in spring, I never met it face to face' as she moved into David's arms. Through the years Spring, especially the month of April, would play an important part in her life: they had married in April, would have their first child the next April, and her dad would pass away that same month. Jane would remember when Fons passed away April 26, 1953 that her dad, William Buchanan, had passed away on that same day fifty years before.

Eddie tapped David on the shoulder. "May I cut in?" He grinned as David stepped back and watched them move away.

Eddie returned Edith to David's side. "Thanks, I needed to dance with your beautiful wife so the girls will pay attention to me. Here I go. Watch me, Edith, to see if it works."

David and Edith watched his friend walk away both hoping he would find a willing partner. When he did they began watching Dwayne and Missouri and their fancy steps as the musicians swung into "Bye, Bye Baby." Right now Missouri was no one's 'Baby' as many of the guys gave her 'the eye.' When the music ended everyone stood back and applauded them. It seems Thelma wasn't the only McKinney sister who could dance.

Edith was one that drew the glances of his friends and those who may want to take advantage of a man who might leave his wife unattended. Feeling possessive of his beautiful wife, he took her upstairs early leaving Dwayne and Missouri at the festivities. By this time she had her own key to their apartment.

This night he would remember; one that set a new direction in his life. They both were eager to hold each other, to make love. Although they could hear the music and people coming up and down the stairs visiting the toilet, the peaceful aftermath had them both falling into a deep sleep. They didn't hear Missouri slip in after stopping in the toilet.

The weekend didn't last long and Missouri needed to go back up the mountain. She was taking art lessons from a well-known artist from New York City, Frank Stanley Herring, who had been coming to Little Switzerland for some years with his wife. They had become friends of her family. He especially liked to have Granny Nancy sit for him but painted several portraits of Missouri, Thelma and Ida. He also did many portraits of the 'summer' residents through the years.

This was also the time of summer when the family worked hard to put up fruits and vegetables for the coming winter. The sisters worked alongside Jane and memories of Edith came to them, sometimes unwanted. They recalled how often she wanted to help and they pushed her away, too busy to let her learn. The weeks went by with letters going back and forth.

Thelma told Edith how much she missed her and Missouri; that she had a job now and stayed with Ida and her husband during the week. They lived in a nearby town so she was meeting new people. One young man was a persistent suitor but Thelma thought he was too young for her. He would win her heart in the end.

Edith McKinney and David Turner
1935

CHAPTER 8

Edith received a sad letter from Missouri. She had gone in to tell their granny breakfast was ready. She couldn't wake her. Nancy had suffered a stroke and wasn't expected to recover. Edith would need to come home. She had only been gone for two months before being summoned back up the mountain. Their years together played across her mind as she traveled. Soon after she arrived, she and her family looked on as Nancy passed peacefully in this year of 1935. What came after would effect Edith for the rest of her life.

In this mountain place, when a person died, their coffin was set up in the front room of the house. Silver dollars were placed over Nancy's eyes to keep them closed. This was a frightening sight to Edith. People sat around the coffin for one day and night to keep watch. They brought great bunches of wild flowers, roses and dahlias from their gardens to surround her coffin and perfume the air. It was August and they would need to bury Nancy fast.

Edith and her sisters' bedroom opened directly off this front room. The large bedroom had two double beds that the four sisters had shared when they were all at home. There was no way to enter without passing the open coffin and Edith couldn't pass without looking at her granny's face. From that day forward, she couldn't sleep when there was a death close by, or even in the neighborhood. She had to have a light on all night until the person was buried. She carried this mindless fear to her children in years to come.

The funeral was held in the church founded by those who started the summer colony. Nancy's home place was close by the church and her family cemetery. She had attended services here from time to time although she was a member at the McKinney's church, Chestnut Grove Baptist Church, where she and her husband were founding members.

Nancy Deweese Buchanan, drawing by Frank Stanley Herring ca 1930's

White Farlan Cottage
Little Switzerland, N. C.   August 28, 1935

Dear Mrs. McKinney

Mrs. Scholtz came by and told us that if it rained you all would like to hold Grandma

Buchanan's funeral in the Chapel of the Resurrection. We are so glad for it to be used for this service, and you are more than welcome to it.

Mrs. Buchanan used to love to attend services as long as she was able to come. The picture of her sitting there in her little chair is still in my memory.

We shall miss her on earth, but we hope to meeting her in the "General Resurrection" with many dear ones that have gone on before.

With deepest sympathy, I am Very Sincerely

Mary O. Clarkson

Let us know if there is anything else we can do.

Sketch of young woman by Frank Stanley Herring *with what looks like a coffin around her. Some attribute this sketch as, maybe, Mr. Herring thinking of Nancy Deweese Buchanan's past life on her death in 1935.*

It was late summer now. Edith took the mail truck down the mountain and then a train to her home. She was glad to see David waiting when she stepped off the train. Their apartment was close by to the depot. She still felt strange walking in this unfamiliar place that had been her home for such a short time.

Like her former home, some of the streets and most roads were the same, unpaved dirt roads. But there she knew all the people and most of those who just visited in the summer. Here, although the men tipped their hats and the ladies would nod at her, she felt like a stranger. She still met some of the original settlers speaking in their native tongue, mostly ignoring Edith and David as they passed them on the street. Being used to having her parents, sisters, and grandmother with her, these months had also been a lonely time. It was good that Edith couldn't see into her future; many of her early years here would be lonely ones.

She knew David hadn't been home long from his day job. In these days, he couldn't afford to miss work. Approaching, she saw lights already on in their window. It was a welcoming sight to her; she had a husband and her own home. This thought came as a revelation to her.

"I missed you, honey." He turned and they walked up together.

"Mama had to come to town and brought some supper since she thought you would be tired. It's warming in the oven." The aroma of food drifted towards them from the open door.

Edith's step faltered. A wave of dizziness caused her to lean against David.

"What's wrong, Edith?" He led her to a chair close by the door.

"Why, I don't know. I've felt a little queasy today. Maybe I'm coming down with something."

Edith began counting next day. If she was right, a baby would be coming in about seven months. There was no going back now. She wondered what her sisters would think.

———— ✣ ————

Another letter arrived. Missouri was in love. She was seeing a young man who had been working close by but was from Hickory, a town near to Edith and David. "Maybe I could come down for a weekend," she wrote, "and Paul could come to your place. What do you think?"

She went on to tell Edith about how she met Paul. "I saw Cousin Carrie Buchanan at the store with this tall, dark, handsome young man. I walked right up to Carrie, smiling at them both. It turned out he was staying with 'The Good Roads Lady', Miss Berry, where Carrie worked. He said Miss Berry had gotten him a job keeping books for the foreman, while the crew worked close by on the road.

"We met up later on a mountain trail where I had my easel set up and was painting the mountains above the house. He walked right up and said 'I bet I can do that' and just lifted the brush out of my hand. I like him a lot, Edith."

What she didn't mention was the 'hullabaloo' about another road that was going to be built crossing this Blue Ridge close by her parent's house. It seems Heriot Clarkson had gotten his way and what the locals called 'the Scenic Highway' would access Little Switzerland employing many while a large portion of people across the country were without jobs.

Missouri also mentioned that Ida and Thelma had been home for a visit and sent their love.

———— ◦∞◦ ————

Edith looked forward to seeing her sister, and David thought it was all right, too. He wanted to make a good impression on Edith's family.

Edith wrote to Missouri. "We'd love for you to come. I want to hear more about your visits to Florida, and Paul. David works during the day, and I don't have much to do but read cook books. (For reasons she didn't understand, Edith wouldn't walk up the street to shop unless David was with her. She didn't visit her mother-in-law either unless David took her by to see his family.) I can get a meal for David now which is a good thing. I have news, too. I haven't decided if it's good or not."

With the letter mailed Edith knew she had to tell David. That night, curled against him in bed, she did. "I believe I'm pregnant."

Silence and then, "How do you know?"

"The signs are there. I've missed my monthly, twice. You remember I've had queasiness. I'll need to go to the doctor. We haven't talked about children, David. I don't know how I feel about it except I know I'm scared."

"Edith, I haven't thought about a family. I guess I hoped that was in the future for us. Maybe it is. I'll ask Dewayne about doctors. No point in worrying our families about this yet."

He turned away and began to breathe as though he was asleep. He was remembering his mother's conversation with him about marriage and conceiving children. When he finally slipped into sleep, it wasn't long before he began tossing and turning. He awakened outside.

Muttering to himself he said "I wonder how I got outside without breaking my neck?" He hadn't walked in his sleep since he brought Edith down.

She was sitting up in the bed when he walked back in the room. It was time he told her about sleep walking. This was the first of the revelations from David.

Missouri's arrival, then Paul, kept the sisters from talking about Edith's news. David had borrowed two straight chairs from the business downstairs to go with the two they had so the four of them could sit around the table. Edith had prepared a local dish for the four of them. As David and Paul got to know each other, Missouri helped Edith to finish up what she came to know as an Italian recipe.

She had a tomato sauce simmering in a large cast iron skillet since early morning; the room was rich with the aroma of home grown basil and garlic. It smelled like nothing Missouri knew about. Taking up a large spoon she began stirring it while sniffing the unusual smell.

"What is this, Edith?"

Edith was putting bowls of noodles on plates for each place on the table and began dipping the steaming sauce over them. Missouri brought one to each of them and they sat down at the table where Edith had a small dish of grated, white cheese and a plate of sliced bread.

"This is spaghetti, a dish a friend taught me to make. She made a point of saying it is a southern Italian dish popular in New York City. I think there must be a difference in northern and southern Italian cooking." Actually it was a recipe she had gotten from one of David's friend's mother. Edith had elevated her to friend status.

She sprinkled some of the grated cheese on the noodles and passed the dish to Missouri. Then she forked some into a large spoon she was holding in her other hand and twirled it into a circle before putting it to her mouth. Putting her fork down Edith clamped her hand over her mouth and ran for the toilet.

When she returned David and their guests were practicing the spoon twirl and getting the spaghetti to their mouth. As host, he had reassured them that the food was good and Edith was having a queasy stomach these days.

Paul was laughing, telling the story about taking Missouri's paint brush from her hand and dabbing a little green paint on a small leaf on the tree in the foreground she had been working on.

"She just pulled up an apron she was wearing and wiped the dab of paint right off, saying you better wait until you've had some lessons I think. Since I'd never picked up a paint brush before, I had to agree with her."

The Italian spaghetti dish was a hit with their guests but Edith couldn't eat much of her portion. Their dinner gave David an opportunity to tell them a little history of the town.

Laughing, he said "It's taking Edith time to adjust. She sometimes feels like she is in another country."

After the sisters cleaned up, Missouri suggested they take a walk to see the sights. When they were on the street she made a point of taking Edith's arm, walking behind the men who were talking football anyway. Paul had played in college and this impressed David.

"What's wrong, Edith? Are you sick?"

Shaking her head no, Edith slowed her pace to get further away from David and Paul. Holding her fore finger to her lips to make a 'keep quiet' signal, she whispered "I think I'm pregnant, Missouri."

Because of the close quarters there wasn't another chance to discuss this surprising news. Letters went back and forth between the sisters as Edith and David learned they were indeed having a baby.

CHAPTER 9

Edith's news caused a lot of excitement and memories to Jane and Fons. They were sitting on the porch swing talking about her letter. He reached for Jane's hand.

"I remember that childbirth can bring tragedy as well as joy."

He would never be able to forget his first wife and infant son, both dying shortly after its birth, leaving Fons and young Lawrence. Jane's family had been set adrift when her husband died, leaving her alone with a young daughter.

"I'm thankful for Lawrence and Effie living close by to us." Jane squeezed his hand as she gazed out over their front yard. "I believe Edith is stronger than you think, Fons. She is healthy and will stand up to life, I pray."

Lawrence and his wife had young children, as did Effie and her husband. These grandchildren were a great joy to Fons and Jane. His son worked with him building houses and working at other construction jobs in this community. Lawrence's and Effie's children were close to him and Jane and would bring comfort and company to them as their daughters were leaving home.

———⦿———

Missouri came down to visit often to meet Paul during this time and the four of them were seen around town. Dwayne saw them having a cola at a local drugstore. He was the soul of tact when David introduced him to Paul. You would never had known he was considered a fast young buck about town and that he had more than a passing acquaintance with Missouri.

In October while Missouri and Paul were visiting the Turners, their landlord told David he needed their space. It was time to find a new place to live. They went shopping and bought a sofa and a crib for the coming baby.

They found some rooms in a large house close to the recreation center that the mills provided for the town. This is also the time David and a group of his friends started working out, 'pumping iron', they were fond of saying.

But before they moved David and Edith went back with Missouri for a visit. It was the first time David had seen his in-laws since he had taken Edith down the mountain. Fons took David out to meet his family and friends. He made a point in treating him as part of the McKinney family. David would learn from his father-in-law and became a loving one himself when his own children married many years later.

Missouri and Jane went down to visit Ida and Harry Hand in Orlando Florida in the late fall of 1935. Thelma stayed with her Dad.

Jane liked to go when she felt she could leave Fons. He didn't like to leave home unless he had to, when his work was away from home. He stayed busy building houses when the weather was good and his friends and family were here. This is a letter Thelma received from Ida Hand when Missouri (Zukie) and Jane were visiting her:

Sat. 3:30 P.M. (Winter, 1935 in Orlando, FL)

Dearest Thelma - Honey it would do your heart good to see how much your mama is enjoying herself. Oh, she wants to spend next winter here and every winter. She is sure having a grand time. When she isn't on the "go" (& she sure is just as bad to go as you & all the rest of us are) she sits by the fireplace and reads or writes. Says she did not know it would be so cool (cold) here. We went to see Mr. McJordan's new Sears Roebuck house this morning- it is so modern and all furnished with Sears furniture and has a large window in the living room overlooking Lake Adair as large as a store window from ceiling to floor. It does not open and is lovely. The bedrooms have windows right in the corner. Harriet and Zukie are rushing around getting ready to go with Julian at 5:00 to Gulf Hammock to hunt. Mr. and Mrs. Godwin are already there. Harriet thought it would be good for them to go with him. It will save gas & they can hunt some. He will come back Monday.

Sunday 10:00 A.M. And your beloved mama has only been up a short time & I gave her breakfast of coffee, toast, eggs and bacon on a tray in front of a roaring fire in the living room. She says I will surely ruin her so you tell your devoted daddy that when she gets home it will be up to him to get up & get her breakfast & serve it to her in front of a big roaring fire in your living room-so he can begin by practicing on you. Ha! Ha! By the way how's the weather up there? Saw in paper N. C. had snow-it sure is cold here. I had to get up at 6am this morning-build the fire, which meant going outside for wood, then I drove to the Court House to take hamburger for the Jail. I am buying the food for Jail now. It is lots of fun and are making quite a saving on cost and feeding, too. (Ida Hand's husband, Harry E. Hand, is Sheriff of Orange County, Florida at this time.)

10:30 A.M. and H. E. has a call to go after stolen car & he is having his breakfast in front of the fire and telling your mama about a scrape that happened last evening while we were in the Court House. She was so interested in the "poor" man Fuller brought in handcuffed. Oh! Oh! Mama is going again-going with H. E. to see about that stolen car-at Lockheart-truth is-I insisted-as well as H. E. for I want her to go and see all she can. Well "Honey Chile" - I will stop so they can mail this morning and you can get it Monday. Lovingly Ida & Harry, & Nellie & Pete & Repeat the cat and kittens

---

Edith went up the mountain again a few days after Christmas. She was five months pregnant but Granny McKinney had died December 24 after a lingering illness. That the winter weather allowed travel this time of year was unusual. Edith was a child when Granddaddy McKinney had died but she remembered that he had died in December, too. The weather was so bad in that year of 1924 his Memorial Service wasn't held until the following June.

Fons told his daughters, "I don't think the memories of past Christmases, when you were excited about Santa Claus and gifts under the tree decorated with your homemade ornaments, will overcome my memory of her death." It was a sad time for his son and all the family.

Fons came down to Valdese for a visit in February to make sure they were ready for the baby. He felt better that they had rooms in a house and Edith didn't need to climb stairs.

Missouri was with Edith when she went into labor in late March. David borrowed a car to take her to a hospital in a neighboring town where her doctor delivered their baby girl April 2. They named her Patricia Ann (and I was called Patsy, Patty and Pat but Patty will be used in this book.) Missouri told her family how brave Edith was. She was actually terrified during the time she spent alone in the delivery room without a nurse or the doctor. This experience was so scary she vowed to never go back should she have another child.

True to her word three years later their son was born at home with a local doctor from the newly opened hospital in Rutherford College in attendance. This hospital occupied one of the buildings used at the college that closed down in that year of 1939. Missouri married Paul a few months after Patty was born, late in the summer of 1936. It was a formal wedding held at the Episcopal Church instead of Missouri's home church. Edith and David weren't at the wedding; maybe it was because Patty was only three months old. Maybe. They moved to Paul's home in Hickory close by to Edith and David.

CHAPTER 10

David was good at hiding his feelings. He tried to prepare himself to the coming changes in his life but couldn't come to the realization of becoming a father. His buddies noticed his anxiety, though.

Dwayne spoke up. "You're in a good place, Dave, with a beautiful wife who is now expecting your baby and content to stay at home." They didn't know what this picture conjured up for him.

He berated himself that he was thinking of possessing Edith the night she thought she got pregnant instead of trying to make sure she wouldn't. Of course he knew there was no sure way to do this. What he saw then was a cage and he was in it. His memories of his mother's life, pregnancies and demanding husband, his memories of the chaos, were all too close to the surface.

These memories would create more problems for their marriage, too. Whenever Edith became upset and needed him to calm her fears, he would walk away instead, thinking only of getting away from her anxiety. Sins of the fathers, but in his case it was his step-father.

But when Patty was born, David began looking for ways to distance himself from his little family. And Edith returned to her former home in the mountains.

Letter from Thelma to Missouri (Zuke):

Little Switzerland, N. C

February 9, 1937

Dearest Zuke,

How is the young lady? You sounded sort of sarcastic in your card but maybe you didn't mean it that way. I know I should have written to you sooner but you ought to know me by this time. It is all most impossible for me to write letters seems like.

What have you been doing since I saw you? I had a date Sunday afternoon with a boy from Burnsville. We rode around all over the country and finally ended up at Linville where we ate supper and danced a little. I spent Sunday night in Spruce Pine (with Ida).

We are having a Valentine dance at the Topliff Hotel (Spruce Pine) Saturday night. Ed Fortner and Oren Phelps are putting it on. They are getting an orchestra from Asheville. Hope it will be good. I am planning to go cause I all ready have a date. Wish you and P. W. could get up.

Mama spent last night at Uncle John's (John Henry Buchanan) house. Edith and I kept house and company just poured in. It always does when Mama goes any where.

Dad spent the night with Jess McKinney. Lewis (son of Effie and Fate McKinney) and Landon (son of Maggie and Rufus McKinney) came over for a while and we made fudge. Landon brought some black walnuts. We had a heap of fun. Edith had on one of her funny spells and you know what that means.

Patty is fine. She nearly scared us to death this morning. We thought she had swallowed a safety pin but decided later that she hadn't.

Ida, Gaylord and Rodney (their baby son) visited us Sunday. Rodney is o.k. He certainly is growing.

Write to us soon, Love Thelma

David had turned to other women after Patty was born, using them, maybe thinking he could protect Edith from his lust. His guilt had him on his knees asking her and his God for forgiveness. He faced Edith and her family, begging for another chance. Missouri and Paul insisted he be checked for disease. He passed. This time of stress strained their relationship with Edith and David. I don't think David ever forgot what he considered their interference in his private business.

They moved to a small house closer to his mother, Ollie. Since David's half-sister could babysit Patty, Edith and David could go out together. He had learned how much Edith and Patty meant to him when he came close to losing them. Then David made a new friend.

They met at the recreation center. David and his friends were warming up with weights when they noticed a man leaning against the wall, watching. He looked strongly built, of medium height, with black hair slicked back from his face. He grinned and stepped forward towards David, extending his hand.

"I'm called Alabama, like the state. I like to be called Pitts, my last name. I just signed on with your town league. Baseball. I play baseball."

David was immediately reminded of Gaylord, his brother-in-law who also played baseball; sometimes his team played against this same town league. They had a new baby boy so Ida hadn't come down with him yet.

The guys crowded around introducing themselves and welcomed Pitts to join their workout. This is how it began but Pitts turned up at the mill with a job close by David's station. They sat and talked while taking a break. Pretty soon David knew Pitts' story (or at least the one he told); how he served in the Navy when he was just a young man, played baseball and football.

David and Edith were attending a dance about a week later when David noticed his friend, Alabama, standing close by the refreshment table just watching. He took Edith's hand and led her over to introduce her to him.

"Pitts, I'd like to introduce you to my wife, Edith."

"Edith, this is my friend, Alabama Pitts. He's playing baseball for our town league."

Pitts put out his hand and drew Edith close for a hug. Putting her away from his body, he picked up her hand and kissed it. "Edith, you married a fine young man."

Turning to David, he stepped forward and hugged him. "Congratulations, my good man. May you and Edith have many happy years together."

David noticed the expression on his friend's face. He was smiling but his eyes weren't. They had never discussed women so David thought the worst. Pitts hadn't been so lucky in love. But then his nomadic life wouldn't lend itself to married life, would it. He never heard that part of his story.

The next time Gaylord's team played Valdese he brought Ida and their son who was almost a year old. Edith had Pitts over to eat so he could meet the good hitter he had noticed on the opposing team. The men talked sports in general after a good meal but baseball was it for Gaylord and Pitts.

Edith and Ida prepared the children for bed before cleaning up the kitchen, giving the men time to talk. It also allowed the sisters time to discuss what was happening with their parents.

"I think Mama and Dad are alone for the first time since their marriage some 27 years ago. With Thelma staying with us during the week and sometimes on the weekend, too, I believe they're mighty lonesome."

"Well, it's good they live close by Lawrence and Effie. Living between these two families the children are all over the place. The last time I was home I noticed they keep them company now. But another thing that pulls on them is the loss of their mothers. I don't think that ever gets easier." This was the beginning of many such times they would be together.

David loved football better than baseball but soon his new friend was elevated to hero status and maybe a father figure. When Edith and David's son was born, Pitts was the first person David told.

According to Missouri, Patty was staying with Fons and Jane when her labor pains started. Edith was determined to stay at home and have this child so a local doctor came to supervise the birth; it was hard labor. The baby was large; no incision was made to widen the mouth of the birth canal and the ensuing tear was unattended. It is hard to think about how painful and frightening this birth was for David's young wife. But Jim came into this world on August 2, 1939, 76 years after his great-grandfather died on the same day in 1863.

Many years later Edith would still be troubled by what happened or didn't happen that day. She found out it wasn't easier to have a baby at home. At that time she would have signs of pre-cancerous cells, leading to a hysterectomy, putting her into early menopause. She thought this happened because of this unattended tear but then in future it might be attributed to her husband carrying an unknown virus transmitted by sexual intercourse.

Pitts was working now as the baseball coach at the high school so he and David didn't see each other as often. In 1940 he signed with another league in Hickory which put more distance between the two men. But Missouri and Paul tried to include David and Edith in their social activities so they saw him now and then.

Then one fateful night in the summer of 1941 David saw Pitts walk into a tavern in town. He tried to wave him down but didn't get his attention. Taking his soft drink that he had just bought on the store side of the building, David walked in behind him where a dance was in full swing. As he stepped in the door he saw Pitts tap a man on the arm, cutting in on him and his partner. He looked up at David standing in the door just as the man drew a knife and stabbed Pitts under his arm. In the melee David couldn't get to his friend. He never saw him alive again. Pitts bled to death from a severed artery.

It wasn't long until David started spending more and more time with his buddies leaving Edith to care for their children: gigging for frogs, hunting, just hanging around with the 'boys.' It didn't seem to matter to him that she needed him more now.

Patty brought her friends to see uncooked frog legs lying in a dish in the refrigerator, quivering when a few grains of salt was dropped on them.

A neighbor child practiced her favorite song, "Mairzy Doats," at the Turner house about this time which she later learned was based on a nursery rhyme, "Mares eat Oats and Does eat Oats and Little Lambs eat Ivy." This was several years before it became a popular song in 1944. It must have been around for some time, though. Patty liked to sing "You Are My Sunshine" and learned every word.

David did sometimes take his family to visit his friends and their parents who were part of the original settlers of this town. Edith had learned to make more of their native dishes that were so different from her mountain heritage.

It *was* like traveling to a foreign country for Edith. Some of these homes were built like those in the alpine area of northwest Italy. One such farming family lived on the top floors while the cow and other farm animals occupied the bottom portion, under their living quarters. These people were warm and welcoming, like Edith's family, offering food and drink to their guests. She remembers sometimes they offered a taste of wine from their own kegs.

Later the Turners enjoyed going to corn shuckings. This was always a family affair and most in the neighborhood attended. There were huge piles of dried corn under a large, open shed where grownups shucked the corn. The children knew how to rub the cobs together, loosening the kernels which would fall into a pail they held in their laps. There was also long tables holding platters and bowls of food prepared by all the wives and there were local musicians.

The music helped keep up the rhythm while working but it also had the children and adults clapping their hands, playing tag and square dancing before and after a large meal. This coming together of neighbors working to help each other made this a community. One that kept families close for years to come.

During this time David never talked about Pitts. It was like he had never been. When his name came up and it often did, David would walk away, especially when they were talking about the robberies or his prison days. Since he never heard these stories from Pitts himself David didn't believe them anyway. In 1942 David enlisted in the Navy.

In the autumn of 1942, when David had enlisted in the Navy, Edith's mind was trying to take in the events of the past couple of years. When the Japanese bombed Pearl Harbor, we declared war on Japan and Nazi Germany declared war on us.

Of course she didn't know his intentions until the telegram arrived. "Go see a Notary at Town Hall. I need you to sign a statement saying you and the children will be all right while I am in the Navy."

The Notary knew what she needed although David hadn't realized the rules might be different for a married man to enlist:

I hereby consent to the enlistment of my husband <u>David Turner</u> in the U. S. Navy Reserve.

I will be able to support myself on the pay of rating for which he is enlisted.

<u>Edith Turner</u>, 11th. September, 1942

But they also had Patty and Jim to feed. Edith got a job.

In the early days of the war, since their town was settled by Italians, non-Italians began looking at them as a possible threat during this time. After all, Italy was fighting with Hitler. There were German families, all American citizens like the Waldensians, who also got the evil-eye. This was a time when suspicions were high; talk of secret two-way radios being hidden but reporting directly to our enemies was whispered about. There was a general unease everywhere but for many having President Roosevelt in charge gave them courage.

The memory of the CCC (Civilian Conservation Corps) camps that trained and gave jobs to young men across the country during the Great Depression was fresh in their minds. These same young men were called into serving their country when war was declared.

David Turner with Navy buddies, Pensacola, FL

Then David and Edith arranged a trip for her to come to Pensacola when his training had allowed him time off. She was to stop in Charleston, South Carolina where he would meet her. Jim and Patty stayed with Ollie. Edith went down by train - a train full of troops going to various camps in South Carolina, Georgia, Alabama and Florida. The 'boys' fell over themselves getting food and drink for her. When a group got off at their station or to change trains, another group pushed and shoved to take over for them.

Edith was the young, beautiful wife of a sailor. They treated her with special care. She enjoyed the courtesy these young men lavished on her; and they gave her their attention when they wouldn't be able to give this to their sweethearts for a long time to come. Some may have remembered Edith's face as they drew their last breath far from their home.

Edith knew David had lost his reason for a while, carousing bars looking for willing women, when the Navy training became too much or that was the excuse he had made to himself. He needed more than his ability to swim long distances and strong muscles for this new program the Navy was putting together that he had hoped to join, becoming a Navy SEAL. His lack of math and language skills pretty much stopped this path for him. He had been training to swim under water, placing or detecting explosive devices on the bottom of ships. Patty remembers him swimming across the Catawba River carrying her on his back with her arms clasped around his neck. Lord, have mercy! He had also begun having pain in his feet as his physical training became more strenuous.

And this was the time David and his brother Edgar had made contact and he and his wife were to meet them in Charleston. After graduating high school in the orphanage and working for a printer in Charlotte, Edgar had joined the Army. When World War II engulfed our country he would be sent to Europe. He had been stationed on Sullivan's Island at Ft. Moultrie where the Army had set up a first aid and supply center. The Navy and Marine Corp had readied troops here to be shipped to the war zone, too.

Edgar had met a beautiful young woman at a dance in Charleston where she had come to work. They both knew they had met their one and only and married soon after.

Edgar and his wife, Mozelle, had welcomed David and Edith to Sullivan's Island. It is located at the mouth of Charleston Harbor and presented a lovely view to everyone and especially to those who had grown up inland. David had kept the meeting a secret from Edith. It turned out to be quite a surprise. (Edgar and his wife became Ike and Ikie to their family and friends. They were called by these nicknames most of their married life.)

The three of them met her at the train station and they rode the ferry over to Sullivan's Island together. This was a special trip for Edith and David. They posed for pictures on the beach in their swimsuits. It was Edith's first time to see the ocean. And this was the beginning of a warm friendship.

Patty, Edith and Jim, 1941

Edith told them all about Patty and Jim and her family. Edgar and Mozelle didn't have children and immediately began making plans to see them when they could.

When he and Edith continued on to Pensacola together David had begun to talk. He had to get his head around the fact that he wouldn't become a Navy SEAL and he needed to find out what was wrong with his feet.

Walking in the sand along the beach had eased the pain but putting on shoes had him limping along. He had seen the concern on all their faces and knew he had to explain. When Edith returned to Patty and Jim she had been thankful she had a job since David's future in the Navy was now uncertain.

⸺⸺∞⸺⸺

Here at home some things people used to take for granted are now scarce, rationed out: gas, tires, and cars. In the months ahead fabric, shoes, fuel oil, rubber, coffee, meat, sugar, even cheese will all take a ration ticket to buy the little available. The scary details of this war would take your eye in newspapers and play out in the moving pictures, not like it was back in the day. You could read about the mustard gas back then, after it was too late for the poor soldier. You could only wonder if his body would be shipped home or not.

CHAPTER 11

*T*he hospital room was silent. The doctor and David both stood as they shook hands. Then he dropped the 'bomb.'

"David, I have a paper here the Navy needs you to sign." He handed it to him to read.

U. S Naval Hospital. Pensacola, Florida,

December 10, 1942

Statement of David Turner, Apprentice Seaman, USNR

I hereby certify that the nature of my present disability, FLAT FOOT, BILATERAL, has been explained to me and I admit that this condition existed prior to my entry into the U.S. Navy Reserve, and that said condition has not been aggravated by service in the U. S. Navy Reserve. (It did not include his initial exam when he was accepted into the Navy.)

"But this isn't true, Sir. My feet didn't hurt before I started training."

"Well, this is required from you, son; a necessary part of your discharge from the Navy." He handed David a pen and watched as he signed it. Many years later David would apply to the VA

(Veteran's Administration) for assistance for his feet but he wasn't accepted. They still had this letter he signed in 1942 in his file.

"Good luck, David." The doctor turned away and then faced David. "Marriage is one of respect as well as love. If you can always think on that, you can go forward." He turned and left the room.

He opened David's file and read: Diagnosis: Fallen arches and recurring asthma attacks, unable to perform safely in battle conditions. He placed his initials above his typed name and closed the file.

It could have read: Walks in his sleep, sometimes speaking audibly, floats above landscapes as he dreams, fallen arches and asthma attacks. It is likely this doctor didn't think it was the business of the Navy to keep records about the signs of his anxiety. I wonder what the Navy would have done if David had refused to sign the paper? He left the hospital the next day.

I can visualize the night David came home.

Edith was tired. It was always hard to get the children to bed but since Patty was starting school it was getting almost impossible. Little Jim didn't like being left with the sitter either; it wasn't as much fun being unable to fight with her.

'Lord, I hope the siren won't go off tonight. As tired as I am I need to sit down without worrying about someone banging on my door.' Just as she finished the thought, she heard a series of knocks, then a voice.

"Edith, I'm home." The door opened. It was David.

Silence filled the room. Edith didn't get up from her chair. David stood a few steps inside the door. A cry came from the bedroom setting them both in motion. Jim, who was three years old, often had nightmares. An occasional siren signaling a mock air raid or a pounding on their door by the warden when he spied a tiny bit of light scared him.

Edith turned on the bedroom light and wrapped her arms around their son as he looked up at David. Of course Jim wouldn't remember him. He had just turned three years old when David left to sign up. He was another little boy whose father wasn't in his life.

"Jim won't calm down easy. Can you wait for me in the living room, Dave?"

David felt a tug on his legs and looked down into large brown eyes. Patty had a look of wonder as she stared up at her dad. "Daddy, Daddy." She stretched her arms to meet his as he swung her up into a hug. She remembered; sitting on his lap while he taught her how to whistle, lying in the floor beside him singing along to "The old grey mare ain't what she used to be, ain't what she used to be" laughing as she stumbled through the words.

"I'm hungry, Patty. Let's go into the kitchen. You probably could drink a glass of milk." He also needed to sit down. His feet were beginning to ache.

"We have milk today, Daddy. This is the day Mama gets a quart from Mrs. McClure. She has a cow, you know. Maybe I can have a small glass."

Wondering what to say to that remark from his little daughter, he walked out of the bedroom with her in his arms and into the kitchen. (I guess he hadn't thought about how often Edith could afford to buy milk). He put Patty in a kitchen chair.

In the kitchen he opened the small refrigerator that had come with this rental house. Seeing a glass bottle of milk and a bowl of October beans he set them on the kitchen table and looked around for a plate and a glass and saw both drying in a rack over the sink. He poured milk for Patty and gave himself a portion of the beans. He found a jar of Chow-Chow and spooned a portion over the beans. Finding a slice of cornbread in the breadbox he started eating his cold supper. 'Heaven' he thought to himself.

Edith patted little Jim as she held him to her body. His body relaxed into sleep again. She eased him down while trying to make sense of David's sudden appearance. He had been in the hospital in Florida but he was here now. She tiptoed out of the room, closing the bedroom door before crossing the hall into the kitchen.

David and Patty looked up as Edith came into the room. Patty swallowed the last of her milk knowing her time was up.

"Go to the bathroom before you go to bed but be quiet. The least sound might wake Jim again." She leaned over and kissed their daughter and watched David do the same.

"Can you close the bedroom door without waking your brother?" They watched her as she walked away, afraid to look at each other.

"You called me Dave. I've never heard you call me that."

Edith dropped her eyes. "People around town call you that. I'm Dave's wife." She didn't mention the way men at the mill followed her with their eyes as she walked by.

"The Navy gave me a discharge, Edith. My fallen arches won't allow me to serve." He relaxed his shoulders but continued to hold Edith's gaze.

"I quit my job for this and now they don't want me. I'll see if I can get back on or maybe get a better paying job since so many men are gone. The doctors think my feet should get back to normal if I take it easy for a while." He watched his wife for her reaction.

Like most of us, David didn't admit to himself the real reason he had joined up. Then in his mind's eye he saw Pitts fall to the floor, blood gushing from the knife wound, his assailant running past him into the night. David failed to save him, failed to stop his killer, and now had failed to honor him in the Navy.

"Jim doesn't know you, David. He needs a father at home."

She stood and began clearing the table. "If we can make this marriage work we need to be together. You won't be called up, then?"

"Regular service won't but I've thought of the Merchant Marines. There's lots of talk about German subs picking off transports off our coast here. That duty may pay pretty good."

He didn't say anything about the reason for the high pay. The Germans were picking off the ships manned by the Merchant Marines acting as transports. Lord help this little family.

"Looks like you have the whole house now. Where's my brother?"

"Don't change the subject. Are you planning to leave us again? What about your feet? For your information, yes, they moved out. With a baby they needed more space."

"David, I wrote a letter to the Navy. I've only received one check since you enlisted in September. It was for one month plus another half month. It came at the end of December. The way I figure it they owe us over $200."

Edith's stomach was cramping up. Her constant stress was already affecting her health. It was a wonder she kept her job as sickly as her stomach was. She wasn't strong enough to stand up to more of David's stunts.

Edith wrote letters to her parents at first. "David took Patty for her school shots while I went to work. Peggy is still coming to tend to Jim but we can't pay her much longer." Then she told them he had gone back to the mill. David had realized his family needed him at home.

David reassured Edith that she would receive what was owed her from the Navy. They did contact her after David was back at work. The back pay request they agreed to but it went through channels. The money wasn't approved until about a year later in February, 1944. The check coming at that time may have had David thinking it was a good time to enlist. He would leave for Norfolk, Virginia in late July, 1944 to join the Merchant Marines.

—— ❧ ——

Edith almost gave up on her marriage when David left them this time. She began looking back on her life; she loved her children but realized that she and David hadn't been ready to marry. She looked back to times when she was in school and winning the beauty contest, recalling the girls she met in those carefree days. Then she thought of her roommate who had won the title of Miss North Carolina and decided to write her a letter that July of 1944. She knew she was 'grasping for straws' but hoped Esther would remember her; maybe they could even become friends. Edith hadn't had money to purchase a group photograph of the contestants back then so she asked her if she had one that could be copied. She didn't get a reply.

—— ❧ ——

David arrived in Norfolk, Virginia and filled out paperwork to join the Merchant Marines August 4, 1944. He had brought a copy of his birth certificate but hadn't brought his discharge papers from the Navy. He sent them a letter asking that they send his records to Norfolk. After following up with a telegram they finally arrived in Norfolk about two weeks later.

But on August 5, David had been assigned duty on the Esso Springfield, which left port that day for New York City. He didn't tell them about his feet or asthma attacks. There was no marching on board ship and he had some training from his short time in the Navy. He was soon riding out storms off the Atlantic. He didn't have much time to think about what he had left at home.

The SS Esso Springfield, according to information put out by the shipbuilder, was a turbo-electric tanker under purchase agreement with the U. S. Maritime Commission. It left Chester, Pennsylvania on April 1, 1944 for her maiden voyage. David's great-grandfather had died in Chester on August 2, 1863, the same day in 1939 when David's son was born.

In 1944 this ship would make eight voyages, the first two having her loading up with barrels of gasoline in Trinidad, discharging the oil in Liverpool and unloading 12 Army Lightening fighter planes. This, her third voyage, she loaded barrels of gasoline at New York and would proceed via Norfolk, Virginia to Naples, Italy. David spent his Merchant Marine tour traveling up the coastline to New York. After 16 days on board he was given an honorable discharge while his ship was loading fuel. When his Navy records arrived showing his medical discharge, it was an open and shut case.

To: The Enrolling Officer, U. S. Maritime Service

David Turner enlisted in the U. S. Navy Reserve as apprentice seaman September 14,

1942, transferred to Navy Hospital November 2, 1942 and was Honorable Discharged January 14, 1943.

This second discharge was a devastating blow to David's self-esteem.

———— ✕✕✕ ————

When David had left the mill again to sign up for sea duty, Edith had quit her job and let Peggy go. She figured she would have to take her little family back to her parents as she had done so many other times when he just left. Then she heard that David had been taken on. He was now a seaman with the Merchant Marines.

She was able to return to her job when Peggy agreed to come back. She knew all about the War Manpower Commission: a married woman could work if she was 21, her children had proper care, and her husband was serving his country. Edith was 26 now. It seems our government had set up ways to make sure the wives and children of our men in service were protected.

Her job wasn't necessary for the war effort but with the shortage of men, all jobs were now available. She hoped to move up from pushing a cart from one place to another place; carrying supplies she had gathered up from lists they gave her, then returning them back to the workers. A skilled job might open up when another man would be called to duty. Edith believed she could learn as fast as the next person. She really didn't know what would happen and tried not to think about it.

A good thing was happening, though. Edith was gaining confidence in herself. She had a job and was bringing home a paycheck. She had actually voted for the first time in the Presidential Election in 1940. The fact that women could vote was still almost unbelievable then. Her mother, Jane, had been allowed to vote for the first time when she was 54 years old. Shock was still felt from this event almost 12 years ago.

The rent on the house was harder to make when David's brother had moved out. Most everything was being rationed and it took planning to have enough food for the three of them. Edith had been thankful to have canned goods from her parent's garden. She had two children and had managed to keep them together while David was coming in and out of their lives. Other than support from her family, she had managed these accomplishments mostly without him.

During these years of going home to her parents with her young children, Jane and Fons had not taken sides. They gave Edith their support but never said a word against David. This had not held true with her sisters.

Thelma and Ida were close by when Edith would come home. Ida and Gaylord had visited them in Valdese and felt close to them both. Since they had a son who was born in 1937 she and Edith had children in common.

Edith met the young man courting Thelma. He showered her and Patty with affection; he knew she and David had a troubled marriage and he had tried to lighten her mood when he could.

When Thelma married him in 1940 at age 28, Edith and David were often subject of their conversations. She had a lot to say about David's antics. She also corresponded with Missouri as well as Edith and they discussed their younger sister and her family.

Thelma and Missouri were living different lives than Edith and Ida. Thelma's life was concentrated on the war in Europe. Her husband was called to serve his country in 1943. This couple had only brief weeks together before he was shipped overseas. She received letters from her husband filled with love and longing. Thelma wrote about Edith and David's continuing marital problems which he had a hard time understanding.

After he was shipped overseas he replied, "Here we are separated by thousands of miles, counting the days and months when we can be together while they have all that we want and can't make it work."

Missouri and Paul had been living in his hometown close by to Edith. They were pretty tired of dealing with Edith and David's constant problems. Their life was different; living close by his parents had given them support and everyone thought Paul's prospects were good.

He had begun taking art lessons from Missouri's instructor, Frank Stanley Herring and Wilford A. Conrow, another nationally known (portrait) artist he and Missouri had met, who also spent summers in the mountains near Waynesville, N. C. Paul developed his talent as he began spending more time at his easel. He was good enough that he could make money painting portraits of influential people in the area where he and Missouri lived. He excelled in painting portraits but he preferred painting landscapes.

From the beginning of their marriage he told Mickey (his new nickname for his wife) he didn't want children. In later years she said he feared for his health and didn't believe he would live a long life. But the letter she wrote to Paul when Patty was born showed that she may have hoped for children when she married.

"Patty has arrived! – Edith's baby girl and I'm so happy! ... Perhaps I should tell you how she looks. Are you interested? Well, I'm so thrilled I just have to talk about it – every great event you know." It sounds as if she cared about Patty and expected to have this experience of caring with a child of her own.

Missouri wrote to Thelma. "Paul is having health problems that will need treating." This was news that Thelma hadn't heard; it came naturally for her to worry about her family so this was a new worry to add to her list.

Early on Missouri noticed that Paul didn't feel well a lot of the time. He tried to disguise that fact but couldn't often enough to keep her fears away. He had already told her about an injury he had while playing football in college and for that reason he had been deferred from the draft. Now there were further developments.

He had talked with a local doctor about his symptoms who suggested he needed to go for treatment; he seemed run down physically and needed to go to a sanitarium where he would receive therapy for his physical needs and the doctor told him he was in such a run-down condition it was possibly effecting his mental well-being.

The place he suggested was in another state. Since Mickey had taken a retail job in a dress shop she couldn't afford to go with him. These circumstances will create problems for another beautiful young woman whose husband would be away. Their more sophisticated friends, some college buddies of Paul, thought nothing of stealing a friendly kiss from her if no one was looking. It took a firm stance from her to keep them in their place.

After some weeks Mickey and Paul were together again. He had regained some of his weight and seemed to have his enthusiasm back for their relationship and going forward with their life together. It wasn't long before Paul was painting again and they were involved with their friends. In their spare time Mickey enjoyed going horseback riding; Paul loved to golf so Mickey started taking golf lessons and there was partying on weekends. She wondered what had caused his breakdown, though. She wasn't privy to what happened unless he decided to tell her.

But Mickey and Paul had a purpose now. Paul had begun talking about an art museum with their artist friends and some of the people who had sat for him to have their portraits painted. The idea was well received and wheels started turning.

This young, attractive couple were introduced to other artists and art dealers by Mr. Herring and Mr. Conrow; it was decided American Art and artists would be their focal point. Legal wheels were turned for an official new art museum to be named with Paul as the first director. Well-known artists gifted paintings and money came in to purchase others. The Hickory Museum of Art was born in 1944 as World War II raged in Europe and Asia.

This was heady stuff for a young mountain girl who had to work as a retail clerk to help her husband get ahead. But in the back of her mind was the worry about her husband's health.

———◦◦◦———

**Thelma McKinney with husband Lawrence
Sparks and friend, NYC, 1944.**

In September of 1944 the family wasn't getting answers to their letters to Edith. Thelma had been in New York where her husband was stationed. He would be shipping out soon.

She wrote Ida that they didn't know if Edith was getting help from David. "She may not have any money or anything."

Thelma had decided to go with her husband when he left for basic training in Georgia. She found a room in a private home where he could come when he had time off. She was able to do this and get a job since she was a trained secretary and could show her experience with her previous job. It had worked well for them and she had a part time job in New York. When her husband was sent overseas she returned to her parent's home temporarily.

Thelma wrote Mickey that David was now home. He had been with the Merchant Marines for just a couple of weeks according to a letter Edith had written her parents. "I wonder how in the world he got out."

They didn't know David had joined the Merchant Marines and didn't tell them about his medical discharge from the Navy. When he realized he had to tell them he sent for his records. Maybe he thought his work so far showed his feet wouldn't cause problems but that didn't work.

CHAPTER 12

David came home from the Merchant Marines with money. He and his brother liked horses so soon after he arrived home David bought a roan colored stallion that he stabled in a garage behind the house. He and Edith would ride together when another horse was available.

"I remember he bought a young mare when Jim was born." Edith told her sister, Ida, who was a horse lover, too. "It seems like when David celebrates or needs a diversion maybe, he buys a toy for himself. It's clear to me that money isn't something he can hold on to or save for the future." This would be a problem in their years ahead.

They heard from Edgar who was now in France. He wasn't expected to be in the fighting lines but David and his family worried knowing he wasn't safe anywhere. Enemy troops were all around with tanks, mortars and planes dropping bombs where they could do the most damage. Certainly a supply station would be a target.

They heard the news that Beulah had married and lived in a small town close enough to visit. She was working as a nurse in a nearby hospital.

David went back to work at the mill where he worked when he and Edith were first married. His time in the Merchant

Marines showed his feet had responded some to the treatment the Navy doctors had given him but they weren't strong. He couldn't stay on his feet for extended periods so his work needed to accommodate this.

He seemed to have made a turn, becoming a family man. Maybe he had made an about face as World War II was winding down. He had tried to do his part in this war but continued to be turned down. He kept moving on, though. David was not a quitter.

Then a nice brick house with some land came on the market just a few doors down from their rental house. It needed work since it had an outhouse, and no bathing facilities. This was strange since most of the surrounding houses had bathrooms.

He sold his horse and made a down payment on the house and moved his family to their new home.

The house needed improvements but there were advantages to this property. It had land for one thing; enough for a garden, and a nice wooded area to build on if the notion took you. It also had a two room shotgun house (a house that has rooms one behind the other, so called because you could fire a gun and the bullet would travel through the whole house) with a screened in back porch. The main house was brick and had a separate garage in the back of the house. Since other houses in the neighborhood were of wood, this one looked as if it might be a step above its neighbors, back in the day, especially with the shotgun house. It may have been the first house built in this neighborhood that is so close to the farms where some of the original settlers lived.

The South Mountains were close by to this neighborhood and as Patty believes the earth beneath our feet have memories, these mountain's memories would remain part of the house when the Turners lived there; where David and Jim worked building a small rock wall around the front and side of the property that fronted on the street. David started this project to keep him occupied as he attempted to quit smoking. He and Jim finished the wall but David continued to smoke.

The house was in a large neighborhood that spread from below what came to be known as The Waldensian Cemetery, which was connected to the Waldensian Presbyterian Church in town proper. David remembered the cemetery area was once called Crow's Hill because of a large group of crows that congregated there. There were several of the original settlers who owned farms hugging the South Mountains close by. But the neighborhood that grew up below the cemetery continuing on down the undulating hills to the railroad below town came to be known as the Crow Hill community.

The mill owners where David worked may have begun building these houses for their workers. The mills started out around 1901-1910 so it isn't much of a stretch to think of a village being built, say in 1920 or before, especially when one of the mills was built close by the railroad tracks around 1913.

David would wonder about who lived in the shotgun house on his property. He thought it may have been used by household help, thinking if it had it must have been some time ago, since the main house hadn't been updated with a bathroom and had been a rental house for some years. Another interesting detail he must have thought of was that no Negro domestic help lived in town for some years before David bought this house but that was a different story.

Negroes of the area had their own school, church and town. Once they or their ancestors were working as slaves; later they owned their own land but are kept separate from white people, free but segregated.

Berrytown, located between Valdese and Drexel, was where they lived and were educated. According to those who lived there education was something the parents cared for and tended carefully for their children. But some remember stories of the time when it was not allowed for Negro children and adults to be taught to read. Here in Berrytown they worked hard to educate their children so when segregation ended, the children would be ready and they were.

———— ∞ ————

David and a friend made plans to lease some farmland between the Waldensian Cemetery and the South Mountains. They had talked it over and decided to plant peanuts, a crop they thought would sell well while the war shortages continued. They borrowed a plow horse and turned the soil, getting ready for the peanuts they would use to sprout when they turned the soil over again. They made a fine crop and when the time came to harvest they pulled the peanuts from the soil and left the vines to dry. But they had failed to consider the distance between the leased land and where they lived.

They borrowed a harvester and towed it, along with the same horse to pull it. They had thought of every little detail except one. When they arrived that Saturday morning, the field had been picked clean. It was a good thing they kept their day jobs.

David also bought a sow that was pregnant, putting her in a covered pen he built in the back of his property and away from the house. Jim and Patty were amazed to see the litter of piglets rooting around for their mother's teats. David thought he would sell them when they were old enough to leave their mother but would keep two for 'bacon.'

But Jim and Patty chose one each as their personal pets so he had to keep these. When the cold day came when David and his friends decided it was time to slaughter them, Jim and Patty learned their fate the hard way with the crack of a rifle and seeing them strung up by their feet, a lifeless carcass. It was a rude awakening to learn how food may arrive on their table.

In February of 1945 Edith became pregnant again. The house may have seemed like a new start for him but this news put David on the road again. That Edith's pregnancy could still trigger such stress and effect on him showed how deeply his early life had shaped him.

No one knows now why he went off to Pennsylvania. Maybe he was taken over by a dream about his great-grandfather while passing the rolling hills below Philadelphia when he had returned from the Merchant Marines. Maybe he had heard that his great-grandfather, David Turner, had died in Pennsylvania after fighting in the battle of Gettysburg. He might have dreamed there were men struggling to walk upright; their ragged tatters of clothing blowing in the wind. Some dropping by the path and left as they fell. David would have thought he was seeing an event from the past and it was personal to him; that the fine line between times past and present was allowing him in. He may have seen his great-grandfather walking to his death along a lonely path those many years ago.

David did travel north reversing the route he had used to return home when released from the Merchant Marines. He never made the connection with the ship he was assigned to being made in Chester, Pennsylvania where his great-grandfather had died. As he stopped along this area he became discouraged and started back home.

Then in April of 1945 the whole country suffered a serious blow. Our President, who had served during the depression in the 1930's and World War II, died. Patty, who was nine years old, was walking along a street in uptown Valdese and overheard someone stop a nearby friend to tell her the president had died. This news would add to everyone's worries.

Here the war in Europe and Japan was all too real. The newsreels were showing atrocities that scared the adults and children. Patty dreamed of seeing Japanese soldiers parachuting down from the sky. In her dream she was walking around the shotgun house on their property when she came face to face with a Japanese soldier with his bayonet drawn. She woke up screaming. This was when she and Jim walked in their sleep for a time.

Then Edith received a reply to the letter she sent to her roommate, Esther, in 1944:

May 4, 1945

Dear Edith,

You must think I'm lost! I see that your letter to Mother in Salisbury is dated July 20, 1944 - or perhaps you've even forgotten that you wrote asking about a group picture which *was taken in Greensboro years ago. I did have a copy (I hope I still have) but it, along with practically everything else, is in storage - has been for four and a half years. After receiving your letter, I hoped that I'd be able to go down and check over several boxes, pictures, etc. so I simply put off writing to you about the matter in hopes that I could send you the picture so you could have a copy made. I'm sorry that I didn't get into the boxes. Everything was in such confusion that I decided it would be best to let them remain wrapped as they were and to pray that the moths and other vicious little bugs didn't molest them.*

I'm sorry about this dilatory reply to your nice letter and I do wish I could have helped you.

Yours sincerely, Esther

(Edith had sent a letter, using Esther's maiden name and it was delivered to her mother.) This was the end of their correspondence. Edith was still hoping to find a copy of this picture of the Miss North Carolina contestants in 1934 throughout her life. She never did.

Some years after Edith's death Patty would learn that Esther's husband, a physician, became a Brigadier General during this war and she lived in Washington D. C. when Edith had tried to contact her. Her husband would become head of the Red Cross and other influential organizations during his career. Both he and Esther are buried in Arlington Cemetery according to her Obituary.

Another Obituary Patty found for Esther may shed some light on what little is known about the 1934 American Legion sponsored Miss North Carolina contest. It states that she was chosen Miss North Carolina in 1934 but her father, a cotton broker in Salisbury, refused to let her represent North Carolina in the Miss America contest that year. This may explain why some accounts say there was no event in 1934.

It was normal to hear Edith talking about ration tickets and ice. The house had an icebox instead of a refrigerator and ice was needed on a regular basis to keep the milk and butter (like their first home). A neighbor delivered it once a week in a wooden wagon pulled by his horse. The street going past their house was not paved at that time and the dust told the neighborhood when the wagon was coming. Sometimes some of the other kids would hitch a ride on the back, at least until they were discovered.

The continuing war created a need for products to replace rationed goods. As she was browsing in the grocery, Edith came across one such item that would take the place of butter. Margarine looked like a small rectangle of lard but had a little square of something yellow to be mixed with it. It was cheaper than butter so Edith took it home to try. She loved cream and butter, though, so didn't buy it often. The product was soon a staple in many homes.

The war put a spotlight on all rationed goods but the shortage of meat created problems for growing children. Patty remembers that Edith bought beef from Argentina in a 16 oz. tin. She made a delicious hash with onions and potatoes. When David returned from Pennsylvania he stepped up to the plate for his family with his hunting skills.

"I'm going to walk up the mountain a ways to see what I can shoot for supper." he'd say before picking up a shotgun, breaking it open to carry then checking the number of cartridges he had in his pocket. He also made sure he had cigarettes and matches, too, and off he would stride.

Edith would just check out her pots and pans and hope he brought something home she didn't mind cooking. Remembering the 'possums' he brought one time had her shaking her head.

When he was able to supplement their diet with rabbits, quail, venison and wild turkeys, Edith regretted the many times she had fretted about his hunting trips with his buddies in the first years of her marriage. She remembers seeing him with Patty, trying to show her how to 'dress' a rabbit. This wasn't a pretty sight.

Patty was in third grade now and Jim would be starting school soon. The past summer had been a scary time for him. Jim had a special friend that he played with and like most little boys they had falling outs and disagreements. Usually they had forgotten about it by the next day. But one hot, steamy day their disagreement got out of hand; they began throwing rocks at each other and one of Jim's hit his friend. He ran home crying.

This was the last time Jim saw his friend alive. It was common for adults and children to go berry picking in the heat of the summer. Jim's friend, who was only five years old, suffered a heat stroke and died after a long hot day picking blackberries. Young Jim was traumatized by his friend's death (and his sorrow of not being able to make up with him.)

Patty's teacher's husband was serving his country. She would ask Patty to take a letter to him to the Post Office now and then.

She would look at the address and wonder about all the foreign places it would travel through.

About this time David and Edith felt confident enough to buy a new refrigerator to take the place of the old wooden icebox on the back porch. They could now keep fresh meat, milk, butter, you name it.

And this was the time he noticed a correspondence course on taxidermy when he went back to work at the mill. He knew he was lucky to get his job back. But he ordered the correspondence course and began learning the steps of transforming a dead animal into a preserved replica of one that lived. It took a surgeon's hands and David found that this delicate work came naturally.

He set up his taxidermy shop in the shotgun house. It became off limits to the kids in the neighborhood. David bought toxic materials he needed to preserve the skins of the birds and animals people brought him to 'mount.' With his talent, he soon had a booming business. He had so much taxidermy work he had to choose between that and his mill job and this was mostly seasonal work so he kept on at the mill. (It has also been told that David performed 'surgery' on dogs and maybe pigs; learning to put them to sleep with ether while neutering them.)

CHAPTER 13

David was jolted awake by bright sunshine coming through a window across the room. His eyes opened and he looked around. He thought a minute, trying to place the room, his bed, or the time of day. He couldn't. He turned his head towards a door opening beside him. A familiar person sat down on the side of his bed, bringing it all back.

"David, how do you feel? Could you take something, maybe some coffee?"

"I can't remember, Edith. What's wrong with me?"

"You came in yesterday complaining of a headache. I gave you some aspirin and you went to sleep. You talked all night, David, about your Navy days, storms at sea, Eddy, Dwayne, but you were deep asleep. You were crying, fighting like. I thought you might have been drinking, out of your head maybe."

"I don't come home drinking, Edith. You know that."

"You've missed a day's work. Where were you, David?"

"I went to find my dad. I took a bus to Salisbury."

Edith just stared at him. "Your dad died all those years ago."

"Yeah. Something is wrong with me, Edith. I needed. ., I needed to see where my dad and our family was when I was born. I went to where we lived, where he died."

"Did you find him then, your dad?"

"I found a cemetery where the soldiers from the north were buried, close by where the Confederate Prison was located, Edith. They came from so many places, and they died right in Salisbury. I guess the railroad made this place easy to transport troops and prisoners of war. I never thought what it must have been like. We must pray we are never foolish enough to go against each other again."

He didn't know that this was close by the place where his dad died.

"David, why do you need to find people who have been gone these many years?"

He lifted his head and stared into his wife's eyes. "I don't know why. I guess I'm hoping to find my place on this earth in connecting with them."

Tears started to roll down Edith's face. "Who do you feel like today?" She reached for his hand.

David covered her hand with his. He kissed her cheek as she turned to him. They leaned into each other as he murmured, "I am your husband. Do you still want me, Edith?"

She nodded yes.

When he went back to work, he felt like a different man but he wasn't. He had finally realized that life is a learning experience; that because he had no example of a family that worked when he was growing up, he had to learn to be a husband and father. When this thought came into his head it had surprised him. He realized that he wanted to become a good husband and father. David knew he couldn't follow the crowd, his buddies. He had to decide his own direction.

It wasn't enough, though. When his step-brother came home from the Army, David and he teamed up as men-about-town.

He was single not like David. As was usual he needed to affirm his allegiance to him (as he did with his friends) before his own family. Maybe he still looked for his self-esteem from his past instead as a husband and father.

Edith took Jim and Patty back to her parents. Of course she wasn't satisfied being away from her house so she returned home with her children. When they came back she found that David had failed to pay the electricity bill and they had no power. He had also sold their new refrigerator, leaving all the spoiled contents on the kitchen table. Edith's family had to help out again.

Thelma's letters to her husband were full of these details. He was now in Germany and wrote of his concern and that he had received a letter from Edith. He considered her one of his 'honeys' since he had seen a lot of her during his years of courting then marrying Thelma. Then they both heard that David and Edith had reconciled once again.

It's a wonder that she continued to let David back in their lives. It would be hard to raise her children alone, yes, but it may have taken more courage to stay with her husband. She would know little peace, never knowing when he might leave again.

And Edith was pregnant. Her venture as a working mother had ended when David had returned home from the Merchant Marines. So they sat down together once more to try again.

Patty was torn when she heard her parents talking about what he had done and the man Edith needed him to be. She remembers him weeping. He felt so guilty that he kept leaving his family and vowed to be the man he so wanted to be. He also wanted Edith to take over their money, pay the bills. This is when David started working the night shift so she had little social life and few friends.

He likely was trying to close off temptations; when you work at night and turn your paycheck over to your wife you don't have many opportunities to step out of line. So he still spent his evenings working beside his friends while his family slept dreaming their dreams without him.

Did he ever worry about leaving Edith on her own especially in the evening? From his own life he knew the ways of men and women. He must have had the common thought that there were only three kinds of women: your mother, your good wife and whores. But during and after World War II, a fourth became apparent: lonely women, and they sometimes were likely to seek companionship. It seems that in all their years together, David must have kept Edith in the 'good wife' category, since he left her on her own most of the evenings of his working life.

Edith and her sister-in-law had bonded somewhat when they had shared a house and Edith could talk to her. As they spent time together towards the end of the war they could also talk about the sad situation with their mother-in-law.

This was a sore topic for both. Edith resented her for what she perceived as taking away David's chances; putting him in harm's way and taking him out of school. It wasn't circumstance with her but lack of protecting your child. But Edith learned through her own life that a mother could do just so much; that there were many events out of their control.

She started using cigarettes. It was easy to accept a cigarette from her sister-in-law but a little harder to learn to inhale. More and more women were taking up the habit of 'smoking,' emulating the beautiful women they saw in the movies. Cigarettes were part of the regular supplies furnished to military men overseas so more and more people had become addicted to nicotine. David had started smoking on a regular basis in his Navy days.

One of the problems for Edith starting up this addiction was that she was expecting a baby. It wasn't known at the time how dangerous it could be for the child; that it could affect birth weight and health of the baby. Patty watched one day as her mother held up a cigarette in front of her face.

"Who is stronger, you or me?" She saw her lay the cigarette down and never pick up another ever again.

This is about the time she received the news that Ida and Gaylord were expecting a baby, too. They were busy these days. He had his own business, and Ida was still teaching school. Thelma would live with them again when she went back to work in their town after her husband was shipped overseas.

<hr />

Patty was fascinated with baby clothes that Edith was hand stitching. As each little garment was completed Edith would place it in a small, wooden toy box. Patty kept opening the box to fold and refold each item. She felt she couldn't possibly wait for the birth of this baby. David kept up the wonder of this event by telling little Jim fanciful stories about where babies came from. Jim was told by his dad that he and Edith found him in a stump. This is where Jim's nickname 'Stump' came from.

It was about this time when David began taking Jim fishing when he was just about six or seven years old. Jim recalls they would walk a couple of miles with their fishing gear. When they arrived at their favorite fishing hole, David would tie a rope around Jim and tie him to the nearest tree, giving him just enough leeway to put his line in but not enough for him to fall in the water. They spent happy hours pulling fish in and would come home carrying them in a pail of river water ready to be cleaned and fried up for supper.

As Jim became older David would take him and his friends camping, teaching them valuable skills that would help them with their merit badges as Boy Scouts. Jim thinks his dad wanted to give them the attention that he didn't get when he was growing up.

When he was older, Jim and his friends spent many summer days exploring a nearby creek. They seined for minnows and kept them swimming in pails of water ready to take them fishing whenever they were ready.

Early in November Edith heard that Ida and Gaylord had a baby daughter. Edith gave birth to a beautiful little girl just a few weeks later, November 23, 1945, while Patty and Jim stayed with David's brother, Garland and his wife. Since it was in the fall season, David had to give up a hunting trip to wait on the birth. Patty was given the task of naming the new baby since she had wished on her mother's wedding ring for a baby sister (although at the time Edith was already pregnant.) She named her Janice.

The first winter of her birth was terribly cold; not only here but in Europe where fighting intensified. Edith had a favorite nephew fighting with the army and she was afraid that he would freeze to death or be shot down. Thelma's husband was hospitalized with pneumonia. He wouldn't be moved up to the front lines after all; he was shipped home when he recovered.

They had a letter from Edgar. He had been posted back to the States for a much needed rotation of troops. He didn't get much rest himself while seeing that soldiers were tended to and that they had what they needed as they were transferred to new posts. But he was able to spend time with his wife and Mozelle became pregnant. They had just celebrated the birth of a healthy son although Edgar was back in France. (Their twin boys would be born after the war ended.)

This year watched the war wind down and many more men die; some of those who returned home wondered if the ones buried on foreign soil were the lucky ones. Edith and David weren't unscathed but they are part of a country that would jump start a new era. They were thankful their loved ones survived.

But another fateful decision would be made after World War II that would affect world peace for years into the future. Great Britain and our country, with its Allies, made the decision to give more Palestinian land to displaced Jews from Europe. The Israeli state was born but a separate Palestinian state was not set up and has yet to come to be. Patty believes this one act and the unresolved conflict has continued the course for Arab unrest and an excuse for hatred directed towards our country.

Edith with Janice, Summer of 1946

CHAPTER 14

The time after the war ended seemed a safe, secure time. Patty loved music and listened to songs on the "Hit Parade," remembering holding a small radio on her lap as she heard Vaughn Monroe sing "Racing with the Moon." In the hot summer evenings she and Jim would lie in the grass looking at The Milky Way which seemed so brilliant back then. Their yard and the cool grass were such a treat while they waited for their house to become cool enough for them to sleep.

David's grandmother, Charity Kiziah Turner, passed away in 1946. He took Patty with him to the funeral in Alexander County where they were able to visit with Turner cousins and their children. Janice wasn't even a year old so Edith needed to stay home to tend her. Jim was busy with his friends and was seven at the time.

Edith's parents were in fair health although Jane suffered with chronic diverticula most of her later years. Fons had some stomach trouble off and on but was well enough to continue building houses. Patty, Jim and Janice remember happy times spent with their grandparents in Little Switzerland.

Fons was still a respected builder as the following letter confirms. This house that he built in 1946 is located off of Bear Wallow Road, just a short walk from the store and post office in Little Switzerland. It would be the last house he would build. He was 65 years old. Fons was diagnosed with Hodgkin's disease in the early 1950's and did not recover.

When Patty discovered the following letter many years later she recalled that she did business with this very bank working in the Commodity trade, not knowing Grandfather Fons had built a house for one of its past Presidents.

LA SALLE
NATIONAL
BANK 135 South La Salle Street Chicago 3
C. Ray Phillips, President

June 5th, 1946

My dear Mr. McKinney:

I regret exceedingly that I haven't been down to assist you in staking out the house and garage, but after all, am satisfied that you, knowing what I am after, can do it just as well as if I were there.

Boggs (the architect) told me that he had been over the land with you and I told him that I hoped you could take on the job and follow it as your best judgment dictated. After you get the plans in their entirety, I wish that you would go ahead with it.

Last fall when I talked with Boggs, he doubted it would be advisable for him to supervise the work on the house because of his distance away from it and I agreed with him, and therefore, after he has submitted the final plans, he will not watch the construction, except as you and I may for some reason ask for it. I am well aware of the fact that an experienced and competent builder very often finds an architect's drawings have to be deviated from

in minor things and I would want you to use
your own experience and judgment without
waiting word from Mr. Boggs or myself as to
a minor change which you find advisable. I
have confidence in your ability and integrity
in having you take on the job.
With all good wishes, I am

Yours very truly,
CR Phillips

Missouri's husband, Paul Whitener, painted a landscape in watercolor of this last house. She said it was the only watercolor he ever did. She gave it to Janice and it now hangs in her home.

———

Janice was a very active little girl growing up. Sometimes it was hard to get her to sit down long enough to eat. But David could take her up on his lap when the family sat on the front porch. She remembers to this day him telling her his favorite story, "The Little Red Hen" while they rocked together. "Porches were very important then; they still are." she remembers.

Janice, Patty and Jim, 1949-50

"Dad was called home from work one night when I swore I'd been bitten by a snake while playing kick the can under the street light (probably a new scratch.) He checked my 'bite' and walked back to work. No reprimand which began my memory of Dad's discipline method."

She remembers her feelings as ones of tenderness towards him and never wanting to disappoint; his way of letting her spread her wings but never clipping them. "He encouraged my spirit and my memory of him is as a wonderful human being and father."

A memory that Patty carries is how tenderly he cared for a deep scrape she had on her right knee after she fell down their neighbor's steps. The bandage was apt to stick to the wound so she would only let him change it, knowing she could depend on him not to hurt her.

As their children grew Edith's circumstances changed according to their needs. David made their 'living' but it couldn't cover extras so she worked at different jobs from time to time; she was a hostess in a new restaurant that Johnny Gardner opened in Valdese in the late '40's, a telephone operator who replied to your picking up a telephone with 'number please,' worked in a dress shop in Morganton, NC, and several different hosiery mills, and last in the school's lunch room in the '60's. Jim and Patty also had jobs after school and on weekends.

Edith had begun working at a mill again before Janice started school. She remembers Patty would walk her to her Grandmother Ollie's house as she was going to school and Edith would pick her up there when she got off work. It worked out well when a neighbor friend started cooking supper for both families, all pooling their money to buy groceries and they would eat supper together in the evening. Janice and Jim were of the age of their children and the families stayed close friends through the years.

This was the time when David and Edith started making improvements to the house. They enclosed the back porch, making a bathroom on one side, and an extended kitchen on the other. David had a large breakfront, and a dining table with benches made for their dining room which was a large room that was their former kitchen. He loved having all their friends and family to eat. (They would bring these pieces to their new house, making a special alcove in their dining room for the breakfront when they moved close by the South Mountains about the time Janice was nine years old,) As they became more settled they made other changes.

David renovated the shotgun house. He took out the partition between the two rooms before paneling the new space with knotty pine. Then he built a large rock fireplace where the front porch once stood. This became the place where be brought his friends and hunting buddies.

**From right, David, Brownie, and friend
enjoying David's handiwork.**

Patty gave Janice her first birthday party here. Her little friends were old enough that some were able to climb up on the roof, while another child was able to climb up so he could swing from the wheel of a spinning wheel (upper, extreme right in the picture) that David had made into a light fixture. It was amazing to watch what a six or seven year old could get into. Patty and her teenage friends would dance to records on a phonograph here, too. Janice has the couch and chairs (that you see in the picture) in use on her porch today. If only we could hear the stories they could tell.

David bought a beautiful set of dining pottery as a special present for Edith that filled the new cabinet. Patty believes this event was precipitated by her accidentally knocking against a rickety table one Sunday after dinner. When the table fell, it held most of their dishes at the time since they had company to eat that day. Most all the dishes on the table were broken.

They also made other changes. Edith and her mountain family had been a part of their neighborhood church as long as she remembered. But during her time in this community she and David weren't settled enough to attend a church regularly. It seemed to her their life had always been in turmoil; he was suddenly gone away and she had children with no father. It was hard to make friends with couples, too, when you weren't part of one so often. This was to plague both of them most of their lives together. But David needed to attend church and he needed to set his life on a stable path. He felt the church would help him do it.

Edith and David took their three children to Sunday school and service. He started teaching a Sunday school class. Edith felt at home in a church that taught a familiar message. So this family stepped into a time when their country grew strong, took up new cultures, solved problems and made them.

———— ❧ ————

Edith had a Buchanan 'cousin' who lived in Valdese. Violet Buchanan Oaks' husband, David, and David Turner had some similar interests: hunting, guns, and history. The two couples developed a friendship that would last through the years.

When she was about ten years old Patty remembers seeing David Oaks and Violet Buchanan together for the first time. She saw this good looking man all dressed out in his WWII uniform walking beside her mother's cousin on a path beside the Hutchins house. The path was commonly used, cutting through from South Waldo Street to the street beyond where

Lowman's store was located. After they were married the Oaks and Turners became pals. It is possible the two Davids met at Mount Calvary Baptist Church where both families attended.

What Patty remembers are their antics when together and their talk of what they got into on some of their jaunts. David Oaks was a dare devil and would sometimes take chances when behind the wheel of his truck. Since David Turner was known to grunt and brace on the dashboard when someone was driving in heavy traffic in later years, there was probably a lot of grunting going on back then. This is when they starting making forays together in the mountains and outlying areas collecting and trading antiques to add to their collections. David Turner collected old muzzle loading guns among other things. He would have them all in firing condition before he was through. Some of them were displayed at David Oaks' fish camp called The Millstone. They were lost when the first one burned.

Sometime in the early or mid '50's David Turner started working at The Millstone Fish Camp with David Oaks. They served up fried fish, French fries, slaw and hushpuppies. To say it was a popular place to eat didn't do it justice. Many still remember the tastes, the aromas of the food and their friends who gathered there.

David Oaks ran for Sheriff of Burke County and was elected in 1962. He asked his friend, David Turner, who was a pretty good cook, to step up to keep the restaurant open and running smoothly. The two couples would dress up and go out to eat, sometimes in Asheville, when the Millstone Fish Camp was closed, maybe on Mondays.

This larger than life man was killed in 1966 at age 44 when he and several of his deputies were trying to apprehend an armed man who was resisting arrest. David Turner returned to the mill to make his livelihood sometime after this terrible event.

David and Edith Turner with Violet and David Oaks at Grove Park Inn, Asheville, NC.

But in the early 1950's Edith's parents lives were changing. A letter from Jane to Ida:

March 3, 1952

Dear Ida,

I got your letter and was so glad to hear from you. I cried nearly two days after you went off (Ida and family lived in Kingsport, TN at this time.) It seemed like you were gone. I got to thinking about you running up and down the road (when you were a little girl) with horse shoes tied on your feet, all of you playing <u>horse</u>. Now all of you are gone. Well, no more about that.

I am feeling bad all the time. Your Dad is doing a little work but can't get any better. Thelma comes up very often and gets our supper and washes the dishes. She is the only one that can come. Well, Ida, I don't know what to do about coming to see you. I want to come so bad but I am afraid to start. Not any of you know what a fix I am in (diverticula). I don't have a minutes ease some days. Your Dad wants to come so bad.

The election is tomorrow and I will be so glad when it is over. Tell Gaylord I do hope he will vote for "Ike" but it will all be over when you get this letter.

Tell Rodney and Ila Gail hello and write when you can. Love, Mama and Dad.

Fons had been diagnosed with Hodgkin's disease and passed away the next year. This was a devastating loss to this family. Patty thought her life had ended. Her idyllic time with her grandparents in Little Switzerland was over.

CHAPTER 15

S ometime in 1955 David bought land overlooking the South
Mountains. It was up a hill from the small creek where he
was baptized all those years ago and close to the place he lived
when he was a young boy. He and Edith had a house built here
where they would spend the rest of their lives. The move to their
new house in 1956 was a symbol of two people (and a marriage)
that had persevered. But the family, Edith, her mother, and two
of her sisters, were going through traumas during this time.

After their father, Fons McKinney, passed away in April,
1953, Jane was in poor health so never lived in her home again;
she stayed with her daughters from that time on. Thelma's
husband fell ill in the mid 50's and Missouri's husband was
diagnosed with a malignant brain tumor. The following letter
from Missouri (Mickey) to Edith dated September 6, 1956 tells
some of the story:

> *Edith darling,*
>
> *I've been wanting to write to you for days
> but have been so busy nursing Paul (at Duke
> Hospital) that I just haven't found time. The
> Whiteners and Frances (parents and sister of
> Paul) went home Tuesday so I have it all to
> myself now. I'm on duty from 7 pm 'til 11 pm*

136

every day. We still have a night nurse. Frances was with me over three weeks but she had to go get Julie (her daughter) in school. I sure do miss her because she was so wonderful with Paul. Mrs. Whitener hurt her side on her way down here and Sunday fell and skinned both knees falling off the curb-could hardly walk so needed to go home.

Sweet one, I'll never get over not being able to be with Mama her last days, and not being able to see her for the last time. My heart is just broken, but when you know that you have to do something it seems there is strength to carry on. I realize that Mama is much better off now. She is free of pain and at rest. However that, it does not keep us from grieving for her. Just try to know that we did all we could for her. We all loved our sweet Mama and took good care of her. Of course we couldn't give Dad and her home back to her. That was impossible and we all have to go through the same thing if we live long enough. (Jane fell while at Edith and David's new home. According to her doctor, her hip just shattered and he was unable to repair it. She remained in Valdese Hospital unable to get up until her death August 28, 1956.)

You have been so brave and good through all this, and have had to carry the heaviest load, Edith. I couldn't help you any more than I did but you realize that it was not my fault. God knows I would have stuck with you had it been possible.

Paul is feeling some better the past few days. However is still being fed by tube and is getting another blood transfusion. This must be at least the 10th one for him. His temperature is normal now for the first *time since his operation so maybe this is the turning point and he will soon be well. If we could only get home. Two months is a long time to stay in a hospital and not know from one day to the next what is going to happen. Poor thing is worn out and so patient about everything.*

I hope you can get some rest now. I guess Jimmy and Janice are in school. Tell Janice she is a mighty sweet girl to write to me. I'm awfully lonesome and mail does help so much.

I don't know when or how I will break the news about Mama to Paul. The doctor said by all means not to tell him now. He hasn't asked about her since she died but every time before when he would inquire, tears would come to his eyes.

There is a lovely flower garden here at Duke and during Mama's funeral I walked down there and set on a rock by a little stream. It made me feel closer to home and my folks. Little blue forget-me-nots bloom along the creek just like they do at home (Little Switzerland.) It was so peaceful and quiet-somehow it made me feel better.

Remember, I love you all, Mickey

Paul did come home and was well enough for a time to learn to paint with his left hand since his right side was paralyzed after his surgery. After a time his tumor returned and his beloved wife nursed him at home until his death in 1959.

During this time Thelma's husband, Lawrence Sparks, was in an accident while delivering laundry and dry cleaning from his business to his customers. His chest was crushed. He had been frail since his Army days when he had pneumonia. He was hospitalized several times but did not recover. These two sisters lived together as young widows in Hickory. Missouri became the Executive Director of the Hickory Museum of Art and Thelma assisted her. After some years both remarried but they continued their work until they retired in their early eighties.

The sisters remained close, visiting each other often. Thelma and her second husband enjoyed visiting Edith and David on most Sunday afternoons. The sisters also met each year with their half-sister, Effie, usually in Little Switzerland.

Almost from the beginning this place near the South Mountains had a mind of its own. Patty and Janice especially had unusual experiences in this house. Jim was soon away in college in the western part of the state. Patty was only a visitor since she had moved to Charlotte to work before it was built. On one such visit, in the early morning she dreamed of a young man she loved. He came to her room where she was sleeping. He sat on the bed where she lay, took her hand in his and told her goodbye. He was marrying someone else. She opened her eyes and she was alone in her room. She almost asked him at a later time if he had a dream where he came to tell her goodbye. She always wished she had.

This is the time in 1959 when she and a close friend, her roommate in Charlotte, made the decision to leave their jobs and travel to New York City and then Hyannis, MA for the summer. This will be the first of many adventures for Patty.

After they returned and Patty was again visiting her parents she dreamed she was looking out the dining room window at the South Mountain range, before the trees grew up and blocked your view. She saw ocean waves lapping over these mountains. Funny how these dreams always placed her in this house when she slept here. At the time she thought this dream might portend an event which might happen here in the future.

The dreams were so realistic they stayed in her mind for years. It was in those later years when her sister, Janice, told her about seeing the ocean lapping over these South Mountains in her dreams. Janice, who grew up in the house, said she had the same dream several times.

More years later they learned this area may have been the end of a continent millions of years before. Patty believes this ancient place had given up its memories to them; maybe even a place where the past and present could come together since all humanity carries the ancient cells of life brought here from the vast universe we are part of.

David and Edith sold some of their property to his brother, Garland. He built a house next door to them while his three sons were growing up. There was room for him to build a stable and corral for his horse. These brothers and their siblings were close as the years passed.

—⁂—

This family has lived in a time when their home town offered schools with good teachers who taught students languages, music, and prepared them for college or business school. Their athletic programs were good enough to send athletes to colleges on scholarships (with a big help from their coaches). Students from neighboring communities were brought in for their high school years.

But these schools were still for whites only. More and more people were becoming aware of what is right and wrong in our society, though; what it would be like to change places with someone less fortunate.

David had grown up with less education and worldly goods than many in this place. His life and Edith's would be molded many years by his early life but in the end they persevered. He somehow overcame his need to leave his responsibilities and became a caring husband and father but continued to smoke cigarettes for many years which would contribute to his early death at age 69; Edith, so young and unprepared, became a competent and loving wife and mother who made the best of her circumstances. She was noticed and admired by a particular married man but nothing came of this attraction. Only Patty knew about this happening. She was troubled by stomach problems through all these years but still kept her innocent delight in being alive and her love of nature and adventure. Both gave their children the confidence to make their own decisions about life's big questions: segregation, religion, politics and personal decisions. In the coming years they came to know that this was rare and precious.

As their children grew up David's and Edith's past years and troubles seemed far in the past. Edith was still a beauty and loved pretty clothes, making many of them herself. She still didn't have many opportunities to wear them, though. David continued to walk the 'straight and narrow path.'

But in 1965 the Turner family is sitting around the dining room table, finishing Thanksgiving dinner. Patty has a husband

(Jack) and Jim a wife (Revonda) and their first child, Jill Elizabeth. Janice was away at school but had managed the trip home. She was eager to get away to see her friends before she had to get back to classes. Having his family increase suited David fine. The more to come home he always said.

The conversation was about David's vegetable garden. A lot of the side dishes on the table came from this garden. He and Edith canned or froze these vegetables, filling up a freezer each year. The two of them were planning new landscaping for the spring season, too, so they were talking about this with Jim and Patty.

What a difference these past twenty years have wrought in this family. Janice has grown up knowing different parents. A stable family life has given her the chance to feel secure and the strength to push her boundaries. Patty and Jim will always need to create their own security, not trusting others to do it. They are individuals from the same parents but different environments.

It was common for them to sit in the yard under the shade of the trees David had planted and under the shadow of the South Mountains when they are all together. David loved the times when they were joined by all his siblings and their families. His birthday was a favorite time for them to be together. This letter almost ten years later from Edith to Patty and her husband in Liberty, Missouri, tells them about one such occasion:

David's Birthday with from left, Garland, Wade, Thelma, David, Edgar and Beulah, Amy. Sister, Louise is deceased.

May 3, 1973

Dear Patty and Jack,

We enjoyed talking with you the other day (May 1, David's birthday). Since we can't see each other often, I think the telephone is a nice thing to have and too, we get a better connection from Missouri than we did in Charlotte.

I think David enjoyed himself over the weekend. It was such a pretty day for a picnic. Hugh (Smith, Beulah's husband and David's brother-in-law) brought him a Rhododendron for his birthday. Jim is going to set it out for him. Jim is keeping the garden worked out real good. He said he wasn't going to have weeds in it this year. You know Jim.

Had a letter from Thelma (Edith's sister) today. She said they had heard from you all,

143

she said she might go out there with us when we go. Carroll (Abee, her second husband) stays pretty busy.

David is doing pretty good since his operation (to repair a hernia). He may go back to work in another week.

Wade's (David's youngest half-brother) daughter, Brenda, brought her husband and baby with her. Everyone likes her husband. He's a redhead and is the type of person you feel like you have known for a long time. He makes himself at home. They have a cute baby boy.

It has started to rain again. The things we planted in the garden this week will be coming up soon. Revonda and I got down to the garden and planted cantaloupes and cucumbers. Our onions are big enough to eat now.

Ike (Edgar Turner, David's brother) said he would come back when the grapes are ripe and help David make wine. Ikie (Mozelle, Edgar's wife) is going to visit some of her people.

Patty, I hope the tornados and flooding is over there. I know that is a new experience for you and Jack but I guess it is a common thing in the flatlands.

Janice called Wed. and said they plan to come home for a few days next week. (Janice, John (Cline) and their family live in Birmingham, AL at this time.) John's class is having a reunion. We will be glad to see them. I talked to the children (John David, Leslie and Shannon) on the phone. They seem anxious to come.

Honey, I think David is going to write you a letter to thank you for his present and I will close for now. Hope to see all before long. Write when you can.

Love you, Mother

David's letter:

Dear Pat and Jack,

I want to thank you both for the check. It makes me feel mighty good to know that you think of me and Mama the way you all do.

You and Jack are two fine people and I am proud you are in our family. I am getting along fine with my operation. I will probably go back to work in one more week.

You better keep this letter. It is the first letter that I have written in about 25 years. Ha. Ha.

With love, Dad

The Turner family and their friends had seen the beginning of big changes in their culture after World War II. The liaison between corporations and our country became more concentrated during this war; quickly it expanded from airplanes, jeeps and tanks to those manufacturing other consumer goods that helped us prevail and brought great prosperity to our country after the war. Going forward this partnership would continue for good or ill according to your perspective.

David, Patty and Jim were part of the downside to this success as they became addicted to cigarettes. Thankfully they were able to stop this terrible habit but David had emphysema by the time he stopped smoking.

It was well known at the end of the 19th century that tobacco was harmful to your health so there must have been some heavy selling going on when all our soldiers, sailors and marines were receiving a constant supply of cigarettes wherever they were.

(And there's a story told that some of the movie actors and actresses were paid to smoke cigarettes as the stories unfolded on screen.) Those who acquired an addiction to cigarettes during World War I and II and after would be part of one of the largest health problems in the history of our country.

In the '60's children and adults were being told by these same businesses that in order to be the man, woman or child you wanted to be, you needed certain clothes, automobiles, etc. which they sold. Of course you needed to smoke cigarettes to be like the people you saw in the movies. In retrospect this was a time of great change in the world.

Advertising of goods for sale will continue to require good decisions by all, though. Every 'new' product isn't necessarily good for an individual or to the society in which a person lives according to the history we have come to know.

Out of sight, out of mind, is how Patty remembers thinking of Negro families when she was growing up. There were none living in town, so unless their parents talked about this segregation, as Edith and David didn't, it was if they didn't exist. But if you traveled by bus or train, you were soon reminded: water fountains, rest rooms, restaurants were for Whites only or if they were lucky, Negroes had separate facilities. It didn't matter that both races fought in the same war, when they came home everything went back to 'normal.

As Patty, Jim and Janice became more aware of their world, they and their friends would become part of a new generation and culture. After World War II the new culture had married women continuing in jobs outside the home and beginning to want to advance their place in society. Segregation would play a big part in their lives going forward in the south as churches in the white community didn't lead their parishioners to accept all people. They would come to see that some wouldn't in the future either. The good news also came in the '60's. Segregation was finally struck down by President Lyndon Johnson.

This generation was also learning religion is interpreted by man, and usually suits their thinking at the time. It didn't seem to matter yet that the Old Testament was written down by men thousands of years before man began to learn so much about the laws of nature and mankind; but in future more and more people would begin questioning what was commonly taught.

EPILOGUE

I n the years ahead grandchildren live close enough that David and Edith always have them in their lives. Jim had moved his family back to Valdese after working in Spruce Pine, Old Fort (where their daughter Jennifer Leigh was born), then Greenville, S. C. and now Morganton where he worked as Personnel Director at Henredon.

Edith taught her granddaughters how to sew, the names of plants and flowers and gave them and their grandson her time and deep affection. David would take his grandson (John David Cline) hunting after showing him how to breakdown his gun and how to keep his cartridges separate until they were in their stand and ready to shoot.

He liked to take them for walks in the South Mountains, telling them stories of his youth while teaching them about the wild life that lived here. And in the future as they grew older they would come for visits on their own, making precious memories and bringing much joy to their grandparents.

David and Edith seemed to be aware of nature and were attuned to it throughout their lives; how Native Americans and other ancient people were respectful of the land where they lived, and why their religions were based on this respect.

People who have visited some of the ancient places in the world like Stonehenge on the Salisbury Plains in England, standing stones in Scotland and pyramids in Egypt were looking at places that were built when ancient people looked to nature and our vast universe to guide them.

⁂

A typical Christmas at their house had David holding a piece of wood under the light, turning it as he gauges its thickness. His hands are beautifully shaped, soft but strong. He laid the wood down on the kitchen table, picked up a pencil and began to sketch a design he wanted for a doll size cradle. He chuckled thinking about Patty wanting this to put under her Christmas tree. 'Too bad she and her husband don't have children of their own,' he thought. 'Then she could put their toys under the tree.'

Edith came into the kitchen where David was sitting at the table. "What are you drawing?"

"This is the cradle Patty asked me to make. I'm going down to the basement and start on it now."

"You had better wear a sweater. It's cool and damp down there." She opened the refrigerator already thinking about preparing lunch.

David noticed her erect posture and her familiar, pretty face. Although her hair is starting to turn gray and faint lines are creeping along her face, she was still the beautiful mountain girl he married so many years ago.

A soft, chill wind blew against his face as David stepped outside. He walked over to the brick barbecue grill, opened the door to the oven, admiring his handiwork. He was thinking of the pork and turkey he and Jim would be smoking in the grill for

Christmas. He looked out to his freshly plowed garden, thinking of the vegetables he and Edith had frozen this past summer, all to be enjoyed when everyone came home for this special time. It was apparent he was a contented man.

Carrying the piece of wood for the cradle he walked down the steps into the basement. Turning on the overhead light he walked to his work area. With careful precision he cut pieces for the cradle with his skill saw and put them together with glue. Edith was setting the table for lunch when David came in carrying the cradle. He handed it to her.

"Patty will like this. I think it needs a quilt and pillow. I'll make them after lunch." She places the cradle carefully on the cabinet.

She began putting food on the table while David washed his hands in the bathroom. When he sat down at the table he reached across to Edith's hand and began to say grace. They looked at each other and he leaned over and kissed her on the cheek.

"I love you, Mama," he said using his pet name for her. She kissed him back.

"Janice called while you were in the basement. They will be here about the same time as Patty and Jack. You and Jim better set a time to begin your barbecue, too. Oh, here comes Jennifer. I'm taking her to the barn for her riding lesson. She is beginning to ride well."

About a week later 'Paw' Turner was carrying wood in to lay a fire in the big fireplace. As he held the match to the crumpled paper, he could hear 'Nanny' Turner in the kitchen setting the table. He smells vegetable soup and the cornbread was almost ready if his nose was smelling right. It was. He heard the oven door open and the ding of the large, cast iron frying pan on the stove. Nanny had been keeping the oven busy for several weeks baking special cakes for Christmas, too. She used to have a big bowl of Jell-O loaded with fruit for the grandkids (until the time they used it as weapons, throwing handfuls at each other. They would remember this, seeing their Paw angry and 'laying down the law.')

"Mama, are you sure the kids will be here for supper? It's beginning to get dark."

**From left Revonda, Jennifer, and Jill Turner,
Shannon, John David, Janice and Leslie Cline.
(Picture of Jim Turner to the right.)**

"Jim will be here soon with his family. Patty and Jack left Liberty (Missouri) yesterday so they should be here anytime now. Janice and her family will be here about that time, too. We'll just fix supper as they come in; keeping this big pot of soup warm won't be hard. I know the children will be tired."

She walked into the living room where David sat on his haunches in front of the fledgling fire.

He laughed. "I know some parents who are tired, too. Remember when we went up the mountain for Christmas? How did we get up there with all that snow, anyway?"

The fire gave out a glow and the smell of burning wood wafted through the rooms. Both were silent as they remembered other rooms like this, the crackling fire and warm, loving faces now gone and only memories.

The silence was broken by the sound of a car door slamming. They both moved towards the front door and out into the cold.

—————

In April of 1985 David and Edith celebrated their 50th Wedding Anniversary at a party given by their children. This is a note Edith wrote to Patty and Jack who were back working in Charlotte, NC:

April 23, 1985

Dear Patty and Jack,

As David and I sat here tonight, my thoughts were on our children. We were watching Senator Ervin and I did watch that for a while, but I kept thinking what a thoughtful thing you all did for our 50th Anniversary. I just had to tell you again how we appreciate all you did. We love you all from the bottom of our heart.

I wrote all the Thank You notes today except Joe's (Joe Mitchell, Jack's brother). That was quite a load at once.

Jim and Revonda planted a few things in the garden today. Jim says Revonda has to take over the garden this year but knowing Jim, he will be right up there.

David is going to bed right now and he says to tell you that you all did a wonderful job on our 50th Anniversary and loves you very much. May God bless you all.

Love, Mother and Dad

**Top: Front Jill, Jennifer Turner, Shannon Cline.
Back John and Leslie Cline
Bottom: Patty, David, Jim, Edith and Janice**

Top: David and Edith with George W. Williams,
Glen and Dot McIntyre
Bottom: Sisters Mickey and Thelma with Edith.

Their grandchildren are now young men and young women who have their own memories of Edith and David; memories that Patty, Jim, and Janice don't share. These memories are of the people Edith and David had come to be. Janice and John Cline lived in Birmingham, Alabama and Bethel Park, Pennsylvania when their children were growing up and Jim and his family lived closer to them.

Jennifer told Patty about some of her memories:

"Nanny and I spent a lot of time together. Paw worked a lot when I was a child, going in after lunch and he came home after I was already in bed."

"I remember her making all our Christmas and birthday gifts for a lot of years. I still have a scarf, a bag, a blanket and two throw pillows she made for me. She taught me how to sew when I was young and didn't show her exasperation when I sewed a doll dress I was making directly to the sofa. She would sew and I would sew with her or read. We kept each other company. I remember learning how to crochet and knit with her. Looking back to those days, she must have spent a lot of time alone with Paw working and when he was gone."

(Sad but this was Edith's lot in life. Her friends had husbands at home during the time David was working and she seldom had evening activities except with her children and grandchildren.)

"I remember going fishing with Paw, Daddy and Jill on weekends. We'd rent a boat at Castle Rock and spend all day in that brown water fishing and catching a lot of crappies. We would come back in the afternoon, set up the Coleman two burner stove on the picnic table on the back porch. I would watch Paw clean the fish. He taught me how but I never had to do it. He also taught me how to remove the bones before I ate the fish. When I do it today my thoughts go right back to him. Nanny and Paw fried endless amounts of fish and served it up with slaw and hushpuppies."

"I lived for Nanny's compliments and would go out of my way to do anything to have her say how smart I was. I thanked her by always picking wildflowers for her and she would put them in a vase to admire them. I believe this is why I have learned all the names of those growing where I live now."

"I miss them both so much. Their home and both of them are always in my heart."

Jill says "Some of my very fondest memories of Nanny Turner were the many times I spent the night and she and I snuggled under her layers of covers. It was such a feeling of security." (Growing up in Little Switzerland, Edith and her sisters slept in unheated bedrooms so many layers of quilts were needed. She carried this need forward in her life because it made her feel secure, too.)

"I also so looked forward to the times she made her homemade vegetable soup. So yummy!

She made me laugh so many times but the funniest of these were the times she would phone the house and ask me to let Sandy (her collie) know it was time for her to come home... like the dog was going to listen to me.

She was such a beautiful woman with an incredible head of hair. I remember cutting her hair, giving her perms and thinking, why wasn't I blessed with a third of this mane.

Pa Turner was such a calm spirit UNTIL the time the grandkids decided we were going to have a food fight with a dish of orange Jell-0 in the kitchen. I will never forget the look in his eyes when he very sternly informed us we were to CLEAN UP THIS MESS!

I also remember the many times he would take me over to the Rock Drug Store for a soda and some candy and I would get to ride in his big light blue truck.

One memory I will never forget was the time he fixed possum and I ate it thinking it was something else. That man would eat just about anything."

And he would, especially if it was game that he had brought home. When Edith would balk at preparing a wild animal he started cooking it himself, sometimes over the fireplace in his "Dog House" with early cast iron cooking pots swinging over the fire. He usually invited his hunting buddies to share in his feast.

———

Janice's eldest daughter, Leslie Rae, who was named for Edith, would stop for an overnight as she traveled close by. "Nanny always greeted me with my favorite pie, lemon meringue

I remember we would sit on the couch together and she would hold my hand. I could always feel her love. Sometimes we would look at her photo albums that she had made, reading her sweet sentiments she had written beneath the pictures of her family."

Leslie remembers how much David seemed to love them. "I liked how he called Nanny 'Mama.' You could tell how much he loved her."

Shannon, the youngest grandchild, has sweet memories of them. "I remember the way Pa Turner sometimes hummed while he ate. Growing up I would ask him to draw something for me. He always would. I remember watching him sitting on the front porch, smoking a cigarette. He seemed like he was in deep thought as he sat there.

I have a memory of Nanny Turner smelling like roses. I think it was the lotion she used but I can still smell it in my mind today. I remember she was soft to touch and always had a comfy spot for me to sit next to her. I'll always remember how she loved to laugh."

All the grandchildren have their special memories they will share with their own children. Maybe they will hear ancient voices tell them about our great universe, the history that we are all part of.

———❧———

David passed away in late January of 1986, the day before we saw the launch of our space ship and its disintegration, and just days before Halley's Comet came streaking across the night sky February 9.

His family struggled with the loss of husband and father. Jim was close by to help Edith. It was hard for Patty to come to her parent's home, though, now that her dad was gone. She and Jack would come by and get Edith and spend a weekend in the Blue Ridge Mountains. Later she and her husband would move there permanently.

Edith made many trips to visit Janice and her family, who now lived in Pennsylvania, and Patty in Charlotte. Jim took her with his family on vacations to New England and local beaches. Patty took her on a trip to visit Niagara Falls which Edith loved. She was eager to cross the huge gorge in a cable car when others were too frightened to do it. She never lost her joy for new experiences and adventures. But even with Jim living close by, when her grandchildren left to start their adult lives, she was terribly lonely.

Almost two years after her husband's death, Edith wrote to Patty:

December 29, 1987

Dear Patty,

I have been pretty busy since you left, trying to get things organized. I have been writing quite a few letters and I went to town Monday to get some cat litter. I have fixed it in a plastic container for Morris (a stray cat she adopted) in the basement. I hope he uses it. (She also feeds him here). He is lying on the couch now while I write you.

I called Thelma Sunday and told her I had come on home with you. She said Phillip, Jr. (Buchanan) and his wife (Jean) were coming down Wed. to the Museum (Hickory Museum of Art) and she wanted me to come so I may go down for the day.

Thank you again for the dishes. Jim came by today and stayed a while after work. He told me Jenny (Jennifer, their youngest daughter) was going to have some work on her teeth before she goes back to college and wants me to be with her when she gets back from the dentist.

I called Carolyn (Edith's next door neighbor) and told her I was home. She said she fed Morris several times and he acted like he was starved each time. He is a big eater.

Well, Patty, I guess this is about all the news I can think of at the present. Hope you are fine and I will see you before too long.

I am doing alright and I hope to start sewing before too long. I haven't been in the mood lately. Love you. Mother

Edith 1980's

Edith's Garden

Edith's Garden

Patty mourns Edith twelve years after David's death. She is sitting in a chair looking at the road going up the mountain past their house turning white with snow. She is thinking that her mother would enjoy the fire burning in the fireplace.

It's January of 1999, and Edith passed away April 21, 1998 after a short illness. Patty is looking at a photograph of her mother made in 1944. Janice's youngest daughter, Shannon, had copies made of it for all of the family. It is sitting on a table that Edith had in her bedroom; one that Patty had brought to her house.

She looks around the room remembering how Edith loved to visit this mountain place. Like her own home she had a special place where she liked to watch the birds. Patty fingers the tassels of an afghan she has wrapped around her; one that Edith had crotched. She feels closer to her mother when she touches the places Edith touched. She would love to sit beside her and put her head on her shoulder like they used to do.

She gets up from her chair and walks to the window, looking out at a place where she and her mother liked to walk together. It seemed natural as she began to speak to her. "I'm making a garden for you, Mama. It's where we used to walk and look at the beautiful view in the curve of our driveway. I'll put a bench there. I had big, moss covered rocks placed there and planted rhododendrons. I went to your house and dug some of the iris and peonies and shoots of holly that you and dad planted. We'll sit on the bench from time to time, Mama, and be with you and Dad again."

—◦◦◦◦—

As the years have passed Patty began to realize how long life has existed on our planet, and the millions of years that have gone by when she and her family and others of her generation weren't alive but then they were. She takes comfort from what she believes:

We are far out in space where time begun. All that was is there. Great mass waits to absorb the breath that life draws here, storing us – our dreams and tears. As dust they drift away into space, caught by dead stars that still shine for you and me and now streak into our atmosphere, bringing all life full circle, to the air we breathe.

Printed in the United States
By Bookmasters